Instructional **Planning**
for **Effective**
Teaching

James H. **STRONGE**   Xianxuan **XU**

Solution Tree | Press
a division of
Solution Tree

555 North Morton Street
Bloomington, IN 47404
800.733.6786 (toll free) / 812.336.7700
FAX: 812.336.7790

email: info@solution-tree.com
solution-tree.com

Visit **go.solution-tree.com/instruction** to download the reproducibles in this book.

Printed in the United States of America

19 18 17 16 15   1 2 3 4 5

Library of Congress Cataloging-in-Publication Data

Names: Stronge, James H. | Xu, Xianxuan.
Title: Instructional planning for effective teaching / authors, James H.
    Stronge and Xianxuan Xu.
Description: Bloomington, IN : Solution Tree Press, [2016] | Includes
    bibliographical references and index.
Identifiers: LCCN 2015033897 | ISBN 9781936763771 (perfect bound)
Subjects: LCSH: Lesson planning--United States. | Curriculum planning--United
    States. | Instructional systems--United States--Design. | Effective
    teaching--United States.
Classification: LCC LB1027.4 .S77 2015 | DDC 371.102--dc23 LC record available at http://lccn.loc.gov/2015033897

Solution Tree
Jeffrey C. Jones, CEO
Edmund M. Ackerman, President

Solution Tree Press
President: Douglas M. Rife
Senior Acquisitions Editor: Amy Rubenstein
Editorial Director: Lesley Bolton
Managing Production Editor: Caroline Weiss
Senior Production Editor: Christine Hood
Proofreader: Ashante Thomas
Cover Designer: Rachel Smith
Text Designer: Rian Anderson

Acknowledgments

Solution Tree Press would like to thank the following reviewers:

Dustin D. Barrett
Principal
Meridian Academy
Meridian, Idaho

Sharon Borton
Instructional Coach
Central Academy and Meridian Academy
Meridian, Idaho

John-David Bowman
Social Studies Teacher
Westwood High School
Mesa, Arizona

Kim Zeydel
Mathematics Teacher
Meridian Academy
Meridian, Idaho

Visit **go.solution-tree.com/instruction** to download the reproducibles in this book.

Table of Contents

Reproducible pages are in italics.

About the Authors

James H. Stronge, PhD, is president of Stronge and Associates Educational Consulting, an educational consulting company that focuses on teacher and leader effectiveness with projects internationally and in many U.S. states. Additionally, he is the Heritage Professor of Education, a distinguished professorship in the Educational Policy, Planning, and Leadership program at the College of William and Mary in Williamsburg, Virginia.

Dr. Stronge's research interests include policy and practice related to teacher effectiveness, teacher and administrator evaluation, and teacher selection. He has worked with state departments of education, school districts, and U.S. and international education organizations to design and implement evaluation and hiring systems for teachers, administrators, and support personnel. He completed work on new teacher and principal evaluation systems for American international schools in conjunction with the Association of American Schools in South America and supported by the U.S. Department of State. Dr. Stronge has made more than 350 presentations at regional, national, and international conferences and has conducted workshops for education organizations extensively throughout the United States and internationally. Among his research projects are international comparative studies of national award-winning teachers in the United States and China and the influences of economic and societal trends on student academic performance in countries globally.

Dr. Stronge has authored, coauthored, or edited twenty-six books and approximately two hundred articles, chapters, and technical reports. His 1994 book, *Educating Homeless Children and Adolescents: Evaluating Policy and Practice* received the Outstanding Academic Book Award from the American Library Association.

Dr. Stronge is a founding member of the board of directors for the Consortium for Research on Educational Accountability and Teacher Evaluation (CREATE). In 2011, he was honored with the Frank E. Flora Lamp of Knowledge Award, presented by the Virginia Association of Secondary School Principals for "bringing honor to the profession" and his "record of outstanding contributions." He was selected as the 2012 national recipient of the Millman Award from CREATE in recognition of his work in the field of teacher and administrator evaluation.

Xianxuan Xu, PhD, is a senior research associate at Stronge and Associates Educational Consulting. Dr. Xu received her doctorate from the College of William and Mary's Educational Policy, Planning, and Leadership program. Her research interests are teacher effectiveness, professional development, and teacher and principal evaluation. She is also particularly interested in researching the relationship between culture and educational issues such as teaching, learning, and leadership. She has presented research findings at various U.S. conferences, including the American Educational Research Association, University Council for Educational Administration, and National Evaluation Institute. She is also a contributing author to the books *Principal Evaluation: Standards, Rubrics, and Tools for Effective Performance* and *West Meets East: Best Practices From Expert Teachers in the U.S. and China.*

Visit www.strongeandassociates.com to learn more about Dr. Stronge and Dr. Xu's work.

To book James H. Stronge or Xianxuan Xu for professional development, please contact pd@solution-tree.com.

Introduction

Planning is the logical first step that teachers consider in the process of teaching: effective instructional planning leads to more effective teaching and learning. When teaching is addressed in a thoughtful, well-planned, and systematic manner, the resulting impact on students is more likely to be satisfying and productive for everyone—the school as a whole, certainly the teachers, and most importantly, the students.

So, what is planning? Simply put, instructional planning is a systematic process involving the necessary tools and techniques to answer the following four questions.

1. Where are we?
2. Where do we want to go?
3. What will it take to get there (time, resources, effort)?
4. How will we know when we arrive at our destination?

Drawing from a variety of traditional planning definitions, key characteristics that apply to instructional planning include:

- Determining present status
- Determining future direction
- Establishing goals and objectives
- Designing actions to accomplish desired changes
- Using methods to partially order events and reduce complexity in decision making
- Identifying the most effective and efficient instructional, assessment, and related processes

All of these characteristics should be present in the planning process to be sure teachers are on the right track.

Why Planning Is Important

Planning is the foundation of most successful organizational action, and this certainly holds true for teaching. To put this basic premise to the test, consider the characteristics of the most successful schools. They have a safe and orderly environment, a clear sense of direction, curriculum alignment throughout the school, excellent instruction, parent involvement, tutoring, and a host of other practices. All of these characteristics of effective schools require a sustained planning effort (Jacobson, 2011; Thapa, Cohen, Guffey, & Higgins-D'Alessandro, 2013).

The same premise holds true for teaching: planning produces results. However, in order for instructional planning to pay off, it must be considered a process—not a product. Instructional planning is not the end result; it is merely the blueprint by which improvement and successful actions are charted.

Effective classrooms are led by effective teachers working to produce worthy results. There are numerous ways in which instructional planning can help make teachers more effective, including the following.

- **Eliminate haphazardness:** When teaching is thoughtful and purposeful, desired results are much more likely to emerge.

- **Encourage a systematic determination of students' needs:** Careful analysis of students' current status and future needs leads to better, more precise teaching.

- **Provide a basis for improvement:** Schools cannot rise above the quality of their people. Moreover, schools improve when teachers, principals, and other employees improve. For their role, when teachers plan effectively, they are much more likely to deliver instruction and assessment effectively and, ultimately, enable students to succeed.

Despite the direct benefits of instructional planning, both immediate and long-term, when teachers proceed without quality planning, poor results are sure to follow. The chain of events that unfolds without investing the requisite time and energy in quality planning is all too predictable. The concept of planning after the fact is an oxymoron. A reactionary mode to teaching is composed less of planning and more of crisis management. Stephen Covey (1989), in his classic text on leadership, *The 7 Habits of Highly Effective People*, describes this mode of operation in his time-management matrix as not acting on important matters until they become urgent. He states that this approach to problem solving results in "crisis managers, problem-minded people, [and] deadline-driven producers" (p. 152). This anti-planning mode results in crisis-oriented classrooms with a constant need to put out brushfires.

How Planning Fits Into the Big Picture

Quality instructional planning is about marching successfully into the future. More specifically, planning should be viewed both as a precursor to instructional delivery and as an ongoing process that permeates all aspects of teaching. Consider how planning can and should permeate all teaching and learning processes, as depicted in figure I.1.

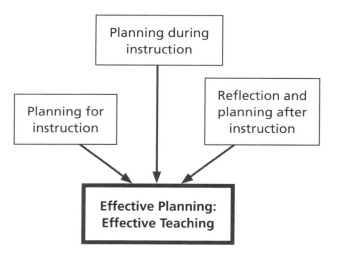

Figure I.1: Planning as an integral part of instruction.

So, what are the right starting and ending points of effective planning? Following are the appropriate steps.

1. Plan thoughtfully.
2. Plan before teaching.
3. Plan during teaching.
4. Reflect on and plan after teaching.

Simply put, the best mantra for the role of planning in the big picture of teaching may be: don't leave home without it.

An Overview of the Book

Teaching is a complex activity that requires careful preparation and planning of objectives and activities on a weekly, daily, and even hourly basis. Part I of this book includes research-based strategies and tools designed to help teachers build quality components in a typical unit or lesson plan. These components include setting learning objectives, organizing learning activities, selecting meaningful and purposeful learning materials, using student learning data, and designing engaging opening and closing activities.

Part II of this book focuses on a variety of broader topics related to planning rather than specific components of an instructional plan. These overarching topics of planning include elements such as strategic planning, planning differentiated instruction for learners at both ends of the achievement spectrum, planning for cross-disciplinary and technology-integrated instruction, and team planning.

To make the book relevant and useful, each chapter includes the following sections.

- An introduction to the instructional planning strategy
- What research says about the instructional planning strategy
- How to move from research to practice

To end each chapter, we include several reproducible handouts to help teachers immediately implement these instructional planning strategies. Our intent is for teachers and school leaders to take the strategies right off the page and put them into practice as seamlessly as possible.

The introduction and research sections provide a solid foundation for what and why the planning strategies should be part of a teacher's repertoire. The research-to-practice section is designed as a solid bridge connecting the best research with best practices.

Most certainly, there are other valuable instructional planning methods and strategies to consider, and while we have not included all possible strategies, we have included those that meet the following two criteria.

1. The strategies must have a solidly researched and empirical background and, where possible, a historical track record.

2. The strategies must be teacher friendly and practical.

Our aim is to provide a set of prominently used, well-researched, quality strategies for teacher growth and development within the domain of instructional planning. As summarized in table I.1, we aim to support three specific groups of educators in the important work of supporting effective instructional planning.

Table I.1: Goals for Each Audience

Audience	Goals of Book
Teachers improving practice	• Self-reflection • Guided study • Teacher-directed growth
Teachers teaching teachers	• Mentor tips • Instructional coaching tips • Peer networks
Leaders supporting teachers	• Directed growth • Supervisor support for teachers • Coordinated curriculum

Summary: So Where Do We Go From Here?

Instructional planning is a process of mapping out what learning targets to focus on, what materials to incorporate, what content-specific instructional strategies and activities to adopt, and what assessments to use to evaluate how students are doing and to inform future planning. Although many expert teachers plan in a seemingly effortless way and rely on their intuition and common sense, such ease derives from years of habitual examination and reflection of instructional planning. Well-designed instruction more often than not requires effortful, careful, and purposeful planning.

Our goals for this book include providing content to help you plan for, improve, support, and sustain student learning with high-quality instructional planning. We hope you find this guide on instructional planning practical, solidly researched, and easy to use. Now, let's put these instructional planning strategies to use in your school or classroom.

Part I

Strategies for Unit and Lesson Planning

Part I of this book includes six chapters on how to develop effective unit and lesson plans. Chapter 1 discusses tactical planning for meeting short-term goals, while chapter 2 offers the nuts and bolts on how to identify instructional goals and objectives. Chapter 3 presents ideas for designing and organizing learning activities, chapter 4 provides guidance for choosing learning materials, and chapter 5 explains how to use assessment data for planning. Finally, chapter 6 provides strategies that help teachers start off a unit or lesson in a provocative and stimulating way. These activities serve to activate students' prior learning as well as jumpstart students' thinking for new learning. This chapter also includes information on creating closing activities that can help the new learning stick.

Anne Reeves (2011) makes a good point when stating that great teaching starts with planning. Compared with other parts of a teacher's job—instruction, classroom management, and assessment—planning is less visible. Nevertheless, this very important task is not any less significant to the teaching process. During planning, some of the deepest work of teaching occurs as the teacher delves into the content and determines how to translate academic standards into specific activities that promote student learning. In this process, teachers not only must consider their own performance—what they need to do, how to organize the classroom, what questions to ask, how to explain lessons, how to group students, and so on—but more importantly, determine in what kind of thinking students need to engage, what misconceptions they are likely to have, and what permanent learning they should take away from classroom experiences. Overall, Part I aims to make the thinking and planning process more visible and tangible. It offers a range of strategies and tools that can assist teachers in developing well-designed instruction to generate and support student learning.

Chapter 1

Tactical Planning for Building Better Unit and Lesson Plans

If strategic planning involves instructional planning for broader long-term learning goals, then tactical planning refers to using specific resources to achieve short-term subgoals that support the defined mission, often resulting in unit plans or lesson plans. Tactical planning considers specific issues that might impact the pace of student learning and growth. In general terms, think of tactical and strategic planning as achieving goals within certain time periods for planning or preparation.

- Tactical planning = short-term goals
- Strategic planning = long-term goals

Tactical planning typically emphasizes stability and reliable, trustworthy techniques; it focuses on immediate needs and improving what currently exists. It drives the instructional engine.

Courses are usually delivered through a sequence of manageable instructional units that accomplish discrete segments of the year's work. Each unit is organized around a specific theme or concept or a cluster of related themes or concepts. An *instructional unit* consists of a series of learning activities and experiences congruent with the intended learning goals and objectives. The unit plan unifies goals, objectives, activities, and evaluation (Moore, 2005).

In practice, a unit plan is often presented as a number of lesson plans to divide the unit into manageable chunks based on appropriate pacing. Unit and lesson planning, in essence, are key components of tactical planning for the teacher. Teachers may want to share tactical plans with students to provide an overall road map that demonstrates where the learning is headed during the term. Furthermore, communicating these tactical plans to students expresses what students are expected to accomplish (Moore, 2005).

To ensure proper coverage of the established curriculum and student learning, instruction must involve careful planning and preparation, with consideration for both tactical and strategic implications. Various studies demonstrate that student achievement is related to the amount of content coverage a teacher accomplishes; in other words, student achievement is optimized when the teacher covers the scope and sequence of subject content sufficiently (Schmidt, Cogan, Houang, & McKnight, 2011; Thompson, Kaur, Koyama, & Bleiler, 2013). Consequently, careful, deliberate tactical planning maximizes the amount of content a teacher is able to cover and, ultimately, the learning students acquire.

What Research Says About Tactical Planning

Based on various studies and reports, effective short-term planning—particularly as applied to the classroom—includes the following elements (Cotton, 2000; Zahorik, Halbach, Ehrle, & Molnar, 2003).

- Clear learning objectives with carefully linked activities
- Lesson plans that are logically structured and progress through the content step by step
- Instructional strategies to be implemented and the related time allotments

- Systematically developed objectives, questions, and activities that reflect higher-level and lower-level cognitive skills, as appropriate for the content and the students

Research indicates that effective and less effective teachers have different insights and approaches to tactical planning. For example, Gaea Leinhardt (1993) finds that effective teachers and less effective teachers have different agendas for their daily instruction. *Agenda* is defined as an operational plan that is concise and focused and describes the intended goals and actions in which the teacher seeks to engage students during instructional time. In particular, effective teachers conceive a lesson along two dimensions simultaneously: (1) the teacher's own actions, thoughts, and habits and (2) the students' thinking and understanding of the content. In other words, effective teachers not only plan what to teach but also keep the students in mind. These teachers anticipate the difficulties students might encounter during learning and incorporate students' needs into their thinking and planning.

By comparison, less effective teachers are not as adept at responding to individual student needs in their planning. They tend to develop a one-size-fits-all approach to planning, whereas more effective teachers build in differentiation and contingencies at different points during the lesson (Jay, 2002; Livingston & Borko, 1989; Sabers, Cushing, & Berliner, 1991). Additionally, effective teachers typically plan a blend of whole-group, small-group, and individualized instruction in their short-term (tactical) plans.

Teachers tend to teach in the manner in which they themselves learn best; however, effective teachers stretch beyond that comfort zone to incorporate different learning approaches and build on students' prior knowledge. For example, during a lesson on the water cycle, the effective teacher might solicit students' prior knowledge, run an action simulation in which students roll dice to determine where in the water cycle they will go next, incorporate a writing experience in which students personify a water droplet and tell about their journey, graph where the droplets went, and then discuss what they observed and compare it to what they previously thought (Stronge, 2007).

Charlotte Danielson (2007) finds that effective teachers understand their students' backgrounds, interests, and skills, which helps plan instruction effectively for all learners. In addition, Elaine McEwan (2002) states:

[Highly effective teachers] are able to articulate the objectives of the lesson, relate [the current lesson] to past and future lessons, and take into account the needs of their students and the nature of what they want to teach. Skillful teachers include components in their lessons that will attract their students' interest and keep them engaged. They are able to mentally walk through their [lesson] presentations beforehand, anticipating where problems of understanding or organization might occur and making adjustments up until the last minute. (p. 40)

Tactical planning involves addressing many important issues and answering crucial questions about teaching and learning, such as, How does teaching and learning build on students' prior knowledge? How can teachers connect teaching and learning to students' interests and learning styles? How can teachers align teaching and learning with their goals and standards? Tactical planning is a fluid process, which is continuously adapted and modified as teachers develop better knowledge of the interactions between content and students.

How to Move From Research to Practice

An essential aspect of tactical planning for teachers is daily and weekly lesson planning. Effective teachers know that daily lesson plans should flow naturally from the unit plan because the objectives, activities, experiences, and necessary materials are specified in the unit plan. Lesson plans also should reflect students' individual needs, strengths, and interests. Lesson planning should not be dictated by rigid standards that prevent and stifle creativity. Indeed, effective teachers rarely carry out a lesson entirely as planned. Rather, they anticipate what is likely to happen as they teach planned lessons and then make modifications as needed.

The following three steps offer practical guidance for converting teachable ideas into a coherent, well-orchestrated daily, weekly, or unit lesson plan—a key element of good tactical planning.

1. Decide what to teach.
2. Decide how to teach it.
3. Decide how to assess instruction and student learning.

Decide What to Teach

Within the guidance and constraints of the established curriculum, teachers determine what content and skills are delivered in the classroom. It is well understood that school district curricula, state standards, and national standards play a role in what students should learn (Jackson & Davis, 2000). However, the teacher's role is to structure how students should learn it. Tactical planning is a deliberate process that results in teachers being well prepared prior to walking through the classroom door for the day (Wharton-McDonald, Pressley, & Hampston, 1998).

Decide How to Teach It

After setting the learning objectives, teachers must design content-specific instructional strategies that communicate content in a way that students can comprehend based on their prior learning and abilities. Additionally, teachers must plan for the context of the lesson to help students relate to the content, making knowledge part of their long-term memory (Marzano, Pickering, & McTighe, 1993).

Having a lesson plan does not ensure that the actual lesson is implemented; rather, a good lesson plan is intended to serve as a guide for good practice. As any good teacher or administrator knows, the classroom is a place of ebbs and flows. Consequently, teachers should follow the predefined plan while remaining open to changes and continuously adjusting their instruction based on student needs. Teachers must also take advantage of the opportunities that emerge unexpectedly within the classroom and tap individual pedagogical and content resources in a fluid and flexible manner to maximize student learning.

Decide How to Assess Instruction and Student Learning

After the learning objectives are established and activities are aligned to them, teachers must link the assessment plan to the objectives. The alignment of learning objectives, activities, and assessment is integral to any instructional design. This type of alignment is referred to as *opportunity to learn* (Gee, 2003; Schmidt, Cogan, & McKnight, 2010–2011). Before actual instruction begins, teachers must decide on valid and reliable assessment techniques to gather student learning data and judge the success of the instructional plan. Effective teachers understand the importance of communicating to students what they are expected to achieve and how they will be assessed after participating in the learning activities.

As teachers design well-structured unit or lesson plans, they should keep the following components in mind, as shown in table 1.1 (page 10).

Figures 1.1 and 1.2 (pages 10–12) show sample unit and lesson plans accompanied by teacher reflections. The plan in figure 1.1, a unit created by fifth-grade social studies teacher Holly Wrighson, is about the Roman Republic. This sample plan includes the major components of a unit plan as outlined in table 1.1, including the matched academic standards, learning objectives in the form of essential questions, instructional strategies and learning activities, and methods for assessment.

Figure 1.2 provides a sample lesson plan developed by seventh-grade science teacher Carrie Alfara. It also comprises the components outlined in table 1.1 under the category of lesson plans, such as learning objectives, introduction, procedures or activities, closure, and evaluation.

Wrighson reflects on her lesson plan as follows:

> I developed this plan for a unit on the Roman Republic. It involves project-based learning in which students use their understanding of the civics, economics, and geography of the Roman Republic to design a provincial Roman city. I also include the draft rubric to assess students' projects. This unit focuses on high-level thinking; students need to apply their understanding of the historical era of the Roman Empire to design a Roman city, and they must include all the key aspects of Roman life.
>
> This project allows students to integrate their knowledge of timelines, maps, civics, economic choices, the government's role, and human interactions. Students also have the opportunity to discuss and revise the rubric, which helps to define the specific requirements and acceptable performance standards of the project. This unit plan involves project-based learning and emphasizes collaboration and shared responsibility with and among students. The rubric activity helps students understand the learning goals before they work on tasks, which allows them to participate in designing their own learning goals and assessments. (H. Wrighson, personal communication, March 6, 2014)

Table 1.1: Components of Unit and Lesson Plans

Unit Plan	Lesson Plan
Topic: Presumably the subject suggested by a course outline, textbook, or state or local curriculum guide	**Objectives:** Specific learning intent for the day selected from the unit plan
Goals and objectives: List of learning intentions in both broad and specific terms	**Introduction or hook:** Provocative questions or introductory activity used at the beginning of the lesson to attract student attention and interest[1]
Content outline: Outline of the material to be covered—with as much detail as needed—which helps clarify the subject and assists with the sequence and lesson organization	**Content outline:** Brief outline of the content to be covered in the lesson
Learning activities: Teacher and student activities—compromising introductory, developmental, and culminating activities—that, when arranged into a series of daily lessons, lead to the desired learning outcomes	**Methods and procedures:** Sequence of developmental activities for the day selected from the unit plan
Resources and materials: List of materials to be selected and prepared for the unit	**Resources and materials:** List of instructional materials needed for the lesson
Evaluation: Outline of an appropriate evaluation plan, including homework, tests, and special projects, that should be planned and prepared prior to instruction	**Lesson activity:** Actual in-class or homework assignments for students, which reinforce learning or help students prepare for the next class period
	Summary or closure: Lesson wrap-up activity
	Evaluation procedure: Activity or technique that determines how well students have mastered the intended learning outcomes of the lesson

[1] Specific techniques for designing hooks might include: discrepant events or common misconceptions; KWL chart (Know, Want to Know, and Learned); interesting news articles or blurbs; real-world problems; controversial topics; and short multimedia presentations such as videos or audio clips.
Source: Adapted from Moore, 2005, pp. 114–119.

Essential Questions:	Common Core Standards for ELA
1. Analyze the foundation of a Roman Republic. 2. What are the foundational values and beliefs of a Roman Republic? 3. How is the Roman Republic similar to our American republic democracy? 4. How did Julius Caesar and Augustus Caesar impact the development of Roman culture and modern ideologies? 5. Why did the Roman Empire fall, and what is its legacy?	W7.7: Conduct short research projects to answer a question (including a self-generated question), drawing on several sources and generating additional related, focused questions for further research and evaluation.

Monday	Tuesday	Wednesday	Thursday	Friday
Learning Target: Learn how Rome ruled an empire and its impact on the rest of the world at that time.	**Learning Target:** Learn how Rome ruled an empire and its impact on the rest of the world at that time.	**Learning Target:** Learn how Rome ruled an empire and its impact on the rest of the world at that time.	**Learning Target:** Learn how Rome ruled an empire and its impact on the rest of the world at that time.	**Learning Target:** Learn how Rome ruled an empire and its impact on the rest of the world at that time.

High-Yield Investment (HYI) Strategies: Using a student-created rubric and a group graphic organizer; design a provincial Roman city, including all aspects of Roman life.	HYI Strategies: Delegate/organize tasks; continue to design a provincial Roman city, including all aspects of Roman life.	HYI Strategies: Teams work to design a provincial Roman city, including all aspects of Roman life.	HYI Strategies: Prepare oral report and rehearse for presentations.	HYI Strategies: Present city projects.
Assessment: Small-group project; Roman provincial cities rubric	Assessment: Small-group project; Roman provincial cities rubric	Assessment: Small-group project; Roman provincial cities rubric	Assessment: Small-group project; Roman provincial cities rubric	Assessment: Small-group project; Roman provincial cities rubric

Ancient Roman Provincial Cities Rubric

	4 Exceeds	3 Meets	2 Approaches	1 Falls Far Below
Research	Students find the necessary information as well as many interesting facts about the city location and culture.	Students find the necessary information as well as some interesting facts about the city location and culture.	Students find necessary information about the location of the city.	Students provide very general information, not specific to the location of the city.
Preparation of the Poster	Students work together to create a clear and interesting poster covering facts about the city. The poster is neat and includes several illustrations.	Students work together to create a clear poster covering facts about the city. The poster is neat and may include an illustration.	Students work together to create a clear poster covering facts about the city.	Poster has confusing text and is difficult to read; it is missing some elements.
Oral Report	All elements of the city are covered as well as several interesting facts. The speakers use clear, strong voices and are able to answer questions from the class.	All elements of the city are covered as well as several interesting facts. The speakers use clear, strong voices.	All elements of the city are covered. The speakers use clear voices.	Oral report is difficult to understand and is missing some elements.
Teamwork	Group works very well as a team. Members share ideas and information and cooperate to produce interesting posters and oral reports.	Group works as a team. Members share some ideas and information and produce interesting posters and oral reports.	All group members participate. However, the work is not evenly shared.	Some group members do not contribute. OR Plagiarism is evident. No credit until revised.

Figure 1.1: Sample lesson plan—Fifth-grade social studies (Roman Republic).   continued →

Preparation	Project is complete on due date; rubrics were used to edit and revise posters and oral reports.	Project is on time and complete on due date; rubric is blank or missing.	Project is late but complete with rubric for scoring.	Project is late and without rubric.

Source: James H. Stronge. Used with permission.

Introduce Learning Objectives
Students will be able to predict whether substances will sink or float by comparing densities.
Procedure
1. **Anticipatory Set: Do Now Activity—Is It Matter?** Students review a list of objects that are considered to be matter and objects that are not considered to be matter. They draw an X next to the objects they consider to be matter. Afterward, they describe the "rule" or reason they used to decide whether something is or is not matter. (This is a quick review of the previous days' lessons on matter.) Call on several students to go to the whiteboard and post their answers. Analyze the answers together, and discuss differences and students' thinking about matter.   2. **Introduction:** Read a short excerpt from the text that outlines information about density and floating and sinking. Tell students this is what they will be learning about today. With students, create a T-chart to predict which objects will float and which will sink. Use the majority of students' predictions for the T-chart.   3. **Guided Practice:** With students, test floating and sinking objects and compare the results to students' predictions. Students answer questions about objects and density.   4. **Check for Understanding:** Circulate around the room as students complete their predictions and questions. This gives you the opportunity to see and hear who understands the concepts and who does not. Use questioning to determine understanding.   5. **Independent Practice:** Students work to form their conclusions about densities of different objects. Is there a relationship between density and floating and sinking in water? If so, describe the relationship. Circulate around the room as students work. Invite students to share out.
Closure
With students, recap the lesson and review the homework assignment.
Assessment
Formative: Use observations and questions to assess student learning.   **Summative:** Use a short preassessment at the beginning of the lesson unit. Give a quiz on Friday, which is designed to correlate to the lab work for summative assessment. (Students predict which objects will float or sink, test their hypotheses, and revise their thoughts based on the outcome of their testing. They explain their conclusions based on what they learned about properties of matter and density [to include calculating the formula].) By comparing the preassessment and postassessment results, you can chart students' growth. Also, students will be able to see their own learning.
Homework
Questions on page 20 of text. Due Thursday.

Source: James H. Stronge. Used with permission.

Figure 1.2: Sample lesson plan—Seventh-grade science (flotation).

Alfara reflects on her lesson plan as follows.

> I developed this lesson—a continuation of the unit on matter—so students can use what they've learned thus far about matter and density to predict flotation. This lesson plan format includes all the components of good instruction: anticipatory set, introduction, guided practice, and independent practice. It also includes formative assessment (check for understanding), preassessment (introduction prediction activity), and summative assessment.
>
> The Do Now Activity helps me to assess students' thinking regarding matter: in what areas they are confident in their knowledge and in what areas they still have questions. I want to ensure that students understand what to do, how to do it, and why they are doing it. As students become accustomed to the procedures, they begin working at their own pace. In other words, this is a teacher-directed lesson. I gradually release responsibility to the students as they become more comfortable with the procedures used in every scientific investigation. (C. Alfara, personal communication, January 22, 2015)

Summary

Unit and lesson plans are the result of careful planning and can be a "window through which we can see how teachers conceive the structure of lessons in relation to their concrete instructional activities" (Shimizu, 2008, p. 943). Unit and lesson plans are basic blocks of instruction that guide students to big learning goals. Dividing the learning process into smaller units and lessons can support the efficiency and coherence of learning. Sequencing and grouping learning goals into units or lessons also help pace the instruction over the course of the year and make progress monitoring and instructional adjustment more manageable.

To close, we provide several handouts to help teachers in their journey toward effective tactical planning.

The handout "Guiding Questions for Planning a Unit or Lesson" (page 15) can be used to guide short-term planning (for example, daily or weekly). The handout provides a number of questions that a teacher can ask himself or herself after planning to make sure the planning process is comprehensive. These concrete questions also can help teachers visualize how a planned unit or lesson might unfold, foresee what might and might not happen during the lesson, and revise the plan accordingly.

The handout "Planning a Unit or Lesson: Self-Assessment" (page 17) is organized around seven attributes of effective unit/lesson planning. Each attribute is unique in its own right, but they all work together to provide powerful instructional planning. Teachers can use this handout to self-monitor and reflect on the planning process. Instructor leaders also can use this tool to assess a teacher's planning or facilitate conversations with teachers about planning.

The handout "Strong Lesson-Planning Template" (page 19) provides a sample lesson-planning template. This lesson plan format consists of planning components that can be used effectively in any teaching situation. It provides a direct and pragmatic template for helping teachers design learning experiences and refine their planning practices.

Unit and lesson plans can be characterized as conventional or alternative. The handout "Conventional Model for Unit or Lesson Planning: Hunter Plan Format" (page 21) focuses on the conventional approach to writing a unit or lesson plan. Conventional lesson plans are developed by setting goals, formulating alternatives, predicting outcomes for each alternative, and then evaluating each alternative for its effectiveness in achieving desired outcomes (Yinger, 1980). Ralph Tyler (1969) was one of the first educational theorists to propose using this style of planning in education. He recommends asking four questions for effective planning.

1. What educational purposes should the school seek to attain?

2. What educational experiences can be provided that are likely to attain these purposes?

3. How can these educational experiences be effectively organized?

4. How can we determine whether these purposes are being attained? (p. 1)

This linear model begins with specifying objectives and ends with evaluating the lesson (John, 2006; Yinger, 1980). A popular example of conventional planning would be Madeline Hunter's Lesson Plan Format (Hunter, 1994, 2004), of which this handout is an example. Teachers can use this lesson plan format to help facilitate the planning process.

The final handout, "Alternative Model for Unit or Lesson Planning" (page 22) offers an alternative model for developing unit or lesson plans. Despite the widespread use of the conventional plan, it is not free of criticism. One criticism is that such linear and objective-based learning is mechanistic and leads to teaching with a restricted set of goals, and it cannot provide a full account of learning and teaching dynamics (John, 2006).

One of the most widely accepted alternative models is the "naturalistic" model, which refers to a naturally emerging planning process. Naturalistic planning involves beginning with the activities and allowing the objectives to flow from the activities (John, 2006). This requires a flow from means to ends as opposed to starting with the end in mind.

One simplified way to use the naturalistic planning model is to select student tasks first, support student exploration of the tasks, and then share and discuss the objectives and outcomes.

For a more elaborate version of the alternative model, this handout provides a nonlinear framework of developing lesson plans—the instruction cycle, created by Eun Kyung Ko (2012). The instruction cycle has nine stages, all of which allow teachers to go back and forth among the stages as needed. This model considers the dynamic nature of the classroom and can help teachers design a lesson plan that shows consistency among objectives, instructional strategies, and assessment. It also keeps instruction and learning from being restricted by scripted materials for greater flexibility.

However, regardless of the format, conventional or alternative, all lesson plans share similar characteristics such as objectives, activities, evaluation, and alignment. Try developing a lesson plan using the instruction cycle, and see how it differs from using the conventional model.

Guiding Questions for Planning a Unit or Lesson

After short-term (unit or lesson) planning, ask yourself:	Notes
1. What are the most important concepts or skills to be learned?	
2. What difficult words or concepts might need extra explanation?	
3. How will you help students make connections to previous learning?	
4. What hooks will you use to motivate students and promote interest?	
5. What materials do you need? How will you evaluate the appropriateness of these materials, considering students' ages and prior knowledge?	
6. What procedures will students need to follow to complete the activities?	
7. How much time will you allocate for different parts of the lesson?	
8. If activities require students to work together, how will you form groups? How will you encourage collaborative and productive work in groups?	
9. What examples will you use?	

page 1 of 2

10. What questioning strategies will you use?	
11. How will you deliver presentations and explanations?	
12. What difficult points in student learning do you anticipate, if any?	
13. What presentation alternatives will you use if students have trouble with concepts or skills (for example, peer explanations, media, textbooks)?	
14. During the lesson, how will you know if students are making progress toward the objectives?	
15. What kind of differentiation will you use if students need extra help or more explanation?	
16. How will you adjust the lesson if time is too short or too long?	
17. What will students do if they finish early?	
18. At the end of the lesson, how will you know if students have mastered the objectives? What kind of product, if any, will you expect from students at the end of the lesson?	
19. How will you evaluate students' performance and provide feedback?	
20. How will you connect concepts or skills to future lessons?	

Source: Questions adapted from Emmer, E. T., Evertson, C. M., & Worsham, M. E. (2003). Classroom management for secondary teachers (6th ed.). Boston: Allyn & Bacon.

Planning a Unit or Lesson: Self-Assessment

	Strongly Disagree	Disagree	Agree	Strongly Agree
Clear Learning Objectives				
A clear road map is set for both you and the students. It informs you about what and how you are going to teach and informs students about what is expected of them.				
The learning objectives are clearly stated in terms of student learning rather than student activity or teacher behaviors.				
The learning objectives cover meaningful and appropriate content, skills, and dispositions.				
Quality Assessments or Assignments				
The lesson or unit is planned with the end in mind.				
The assessments or assignments are aligned with the goals and objectives.				
The assessments or assignments make strong connections to goals cross the curriculum.				
The assessments or assignments allow for multiple ways to demonstrate learning.				
Logically Structured Lessons				
The lessons are developed in sequence rather than in isolation.				
The sequence of lessons and learning activities allows for flexibility and adjustments when needed.				
The lessons build on students' prior learning.				
The sequence allows all aspects of the unit or lesson to be presented in order.				
The learning objectives, activities, and evaluation are aligned and coherent with one another.				

Instructional Planning for Effective Teaching © 2016 J. H. Stronge • solution-tree.com
Visit **go.solution-tree.com/instruction** to download this page.

	Strongly Disagree	Disagree	Agree	Strongly Agree
Instructional Strategies				
A variety of instructional strategies are selected to increase student engagement and maximize learning.				
There is a balance between practicing, drilling, lecturing, problem solving, and questioning.				
The learning objectives and the instructional strategies are aligned.				
Timing				
Proper pacing is anticipated and included in the timing for lesson delivery.				
The amount of time students spend engaged in the act of learning is maximized.				
Appropriate time is allocated for each segment of the unit or lesson.				
Learning Differences				
The variety of instructional strategies selected allows all students to have equal opportunities to learn and master the objectives.				
Student differences in learning are accounted for in the planning.				
The procedures have a differentiation component so that all students' needs can be met.				
Age- and Content-Appropriate Plans				
Ideas are modified and adapted to meet the developmental levels of all students.				
Authentic materials and activities are provided so students can develop the ability to interact with issues in their world that they find interesting and familiar.				

Stronge Lesson-Planning Template

Teacher: _____

Date: _____

Subject or Content: _____

Standards Addressed: _____

1. Learning Intention

Learning Objective: As a result of this lesson, students will demonstrate their knowledge of _____ in the following ways.

Lesson Intention: Articulate the learning intention from the student perspective (student-friendly language, including purpose and connection to the real world).

Today I will learn . . .

I can . . .

This is important because . . .

2. Build on Prior Knowledge

Strategies to determine students' prerequisite knowledge (for example, questions, KWLH, think-pair-share, enter ticket)

3. The Hook

Strategies to motivate students to engage in this lesson

4. Differentiated Instruction

Opportunities to differentiate instruction within this lesson (including what information will be used to create differentiated groups)

5. Lesson Outline

Activity	Materials/resources	Questions to ask during this activity
Guided Practice		
Independent Practice		

page 1 of 2

Instructional Planning for Effective Teaching © 2016 J. H. Stronge • solution-tree.com
Visit **go.solution-tree.com/instruction** to download this page.

6. Assessment of and for Learning

How will I determine student understanding during the lesson?	How will I determine whether the lesson objective has been accomplished? This should relate to the stated learning intention.

7. Lesson Summary and Closure

Summary activity	Closure questions to ask during this activity

8. Reflection

What questions will I ask myself to determine if the lesson was a success?

1.

2.

3.

4.

5.

Conventional Model for Unit or Lesson Planning: Hunter Plan Format

Anticipatory Set: Activate prior knowledge to relate to the current lesson.	
Objective or Purpose: Clarify what students should know and be able to do.	
Instructional Input: Provide explanations and demonstrations to impart knowledge to students.	
Model: Demonstrate the skill or competence so students can see what it looks like in action.	
Check for Understanding: Use questions, observations, and other techniques to check student understanding.	
Guided Practice: Implement activities that students perform under your supervision.	
Independent Practice: Implement activities that students perform without your supervision.	

Sources: Adapted from Hunter, M. (1994). Enhancing teaching. *New York: Macmillan College; Hunter, R. (2004).* Mastery teaching. *Thousand Oaks, CA: Corwin Press.*

Alternative Model for Unit or Lesson Planning

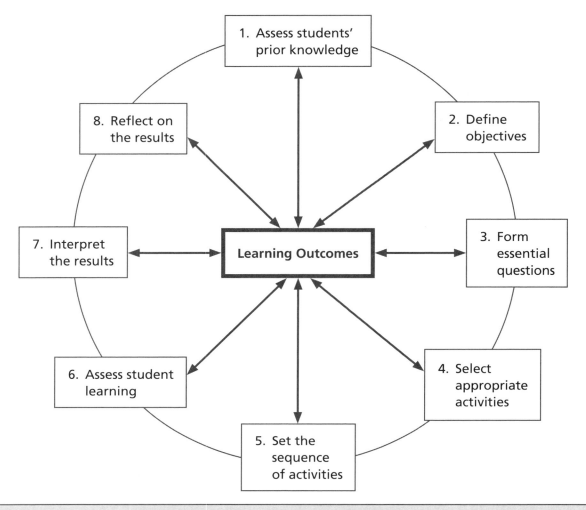

Planning Components
Learning outcomes:
Assess students' prior knowledge:
Define objectives:
Form essential questions:
Select appropriate activities:
Set the sequence of activities:
Assess student learning:
Interpret the results:
Reflect on the results:

Source: Adapted from Ko, E. K. (2012). What is your objective? Preservice teachers' views and practice of instructional planning. International Journal of Learning, 18*(7), 89–100.*

Chapter 2
Setting Learning Objectives

Learning objectives are statements that describe what students are expected to achieve as a result of instruction. The concept of objectives was first used during World War II as a way to make teaching and learning more efficient. In the late 1950s and 1960s, this idea was applied to public schools (Ohio University Heritage College of Osteopathic Medicine, n.d.). In 1962, with the publication of Robert Mager's (1997) landmark work *Preparing Instructional Objectives*, a broad-based movement to use learning objectives in schools began. Generally, the value of identifying and describing learning objectives has long been supported. Specifically, learning objectives have been described as possessing the following key functions (Duchastel & Merrill, 1973; Instructional Assessment Resources, 2011): direction for teaching, facilitation of learning, and guidance in evaluation.

Learning Objectives:

- Can help teachers determine appropriate instructional strategies and activities. They can be used for pretesting, redirecting remedial work of those who lack the prerequisites, and redirecting advanced work for those who already have acquired the objectives.

- Can make the teaching-learning process definite, specific, and goal directed. They provide information about what is to be learned and the way in which students demonstrate adequate learning. Additionally, students can use objectives to guide their learning efforts.

- Can set the framework for evaluating student learning and teacher instruction. They can form the basis for grading or for determining levels of competence in a mastery learning system.

Learning objectives are clear, specific, and unambiguous descriptions of instructional intent. Additionally, learning objectives are purposefully designed to organize learning activities, permit students to study more efficiently, reduce time wasted on irrelevancies, and provide a benchmark against which students can objectively evaluate their own progress.

What Research Says About Learning Objectives

Learning objectives are deliberately designed to facilitate learning and help generate expectations for learning. A substantial number of empirical studies on learning objectives were conducted in the 1970s, and the research overall has been positive. One of these early research reviews by James Hartley and Ivor K. Davies (1976) finds that:

- Learning objectives work best when they are saliently related to the instructional task

- Disclosing learning objectives to students prior to traditional teaching practices (for example, direct instruction) is more advantageous than disclosing prior to nontraditional teaching instructions (for example, discovery learning, inquiry learning)

- Learning objectives do not seem to be beneficial to tasks calling for low cognitive levels of student learning (for example, knowledge and comprehension); however, they are more useful in high-level learning calling for analysis, synthesis, and evaluation

Robert Kaplan and Francine Simmons's (1974) study attempts to determine if it is more beneficial to present learning objectives before a reading task as orienting stimuli for selective attention or after the task as a summary or review? Three hundred tenth through twelfth graders participated in this experimental study. Student learning of information relevant to an objective was relatively high whether the objectives were presented before or after reading the text. However, learning incidental material (for example, information not relevant to an objective) was greater for learning objectives presented after reading than before.

Drawing from a meta-analysis on learning objectives, Karl Klauer (1984) notes the following key findings: providing learning objectives, learning directions, or questions before reading an instructional text leads to some improvement in the learning of goal-relevant material; however, these preinstructional acts impede the learning of goal-irrelevant material. Nevertheless, the overall effect of objectives on learning is positive. Students provided with objectives spend more time engaged in the learning task.

In another meta-analysis, the researcher finds that learning objectives can enhance learning, whether the objectives are presented before learning for orientation purposes or after learning for reinforcing and reviewing purposes (Melton, 1978).

A variety of complex conditions determine whether learning objectives enhance relevant learning and depress or enhance incidental learning. This means the conditions under which learning objectives are used are significant for their effectiveness. These conditions include student awareness of and interest in the stated objectives; the clarity, difficulty, and number of objectives; and whether the objectives are integrated with related instructional materials and activities (Melton, 1978).

Deborah Reed (2012) confirms that teachers' communication of objectives plays a crucial role. She finds that when teachers clearly communicate and reinforce objectives during instruction, students show deeper and more lasting learning than they do when teachers do not communicate the objectives clearly. In addition, when students are aware of the connection between an activity and the lesson objective, it can guide their work and support their learning. Being purposeful is the key. These points are particularly important considerations in *planning* for the use of learning objectives.

How to Move From Research to Practice

A well-established guide for designing student learning objectives is the revised Bloom's taxonomy of cognitive objectives (Anderson & Krathwohl, 2001). The taxonomy is particularly useful for developing tiered objectives based on various cognitive levels, as shown in table 2.1.

Table 2.1: Learning Objectives Aligned With the Cognitive Taxonomy

Cognitive Level	Definition	Performance Verbs
Knowledge	Recall previously learned materials, including terminology, basic concepts and principles, and specific facts	Define, write, state, list, name, recall, recognize, label, underline, select, match, reproduce, identify
Comprehension	Demonstrate understanding of facts and ideas	Identify, justify, select, indicate, illustrate, describe, represent, summarize, paraphrase, name, give examples, translate, convert, formulate, rewrite, explain, sequence, judge, compare, contrast, classify
Application	Use learned information and techniques in new settings	Predict, choose, apply, prepare, produce, construct, select, show, assess, explain, locate, demonstrate, perform, use, compute, solve, operate, manipulate
Analysis	Break learned information into parts to analyze individual elements and relationships	Analyze, relate, identify, conclude, differentiate, compare, divide, contrast, criticize, debate, inspect, break down, justify, illustrate, generalize, deconstruct, discriminate, infer
Evaluation	Make judgments about the value of information and ideas	Judge, evaluate, assess, defend, prioritize, rank, determine, research, critique, explain, justify, support, criticize, appraise, revise
Creation	Generate new ideas, products, or ways of viewing things	Assemble, combine, compose, construct, design, develop, devise, formulate, generate, plan, set up, synthesize, tell, write

Source: Adapted from Anderson & Krathwohl, 2001.

Trifold Learning Objectives

The economy and society in the 21st century require younger generations not only to achieve academic success, career preparation, or civic engagement but rather a combination of all of these. Teachers must create engaging opportunities for all students to develop the knowledge, skills, and attitudes necessary to thrive in an information economy and in diverse communities (Ark & Schneider, 2014). In general, 21st century skills refers to "a broad set of knowledge, skills, work habits, and character traits that are believed—by educators, education innovators, college professors, employers, and others—to be critically important to success in today's world, particularly in collegiate programs and modern careers" (Ark & Schneider, 2014, p. 7).

Without the consideration of all three objectives—knowledge, skills, and attitudes—instructional planning is incomplete. Imagine the relationship among these three objectives, as depicted in figure 2.1.

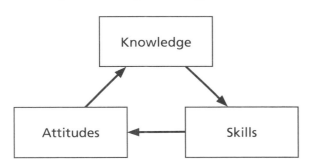

Figure 2.1: Trifold learning objectives.

The practice of identifying three sets of objectives for learning—knowledge, skills, and attitudes—becomes more significant in modern instruction. Actually, this practice of lesson planning has been adopted in other countries, such as China, for quite a long time. This stands in contrast to the more conventional method of the single content objective.

Here, *knowledge* not only refers to the core subjects as defined in policy and legislation (for example, No Child Left Behind) but also to the content of global awareness; financial, economic, business, and entrepreneurial literacy; civic literacy; health literacy; and environmental literacy as outlined by the Partnership for 21st Century Skills (2009).

These *skills* refer to more than the traditional three Rs (reading, writing, and arithmetic); rather, they expand to include higher-order and complex skills, such as the four Cs of creativity, critical thinking, communication,

and collaboration. Skill objectives should include problem solving, critical thinking, forming hypotheses, evaluating, collecting data, summarizing, comparing and contrasting, inducing and deducing, and so on. The skill objectives also should include interpersonal skills, such as responsibility, cooperation, and conflict resolution. When planning for skills learning, teachers must emphasize modeling the skills for accomplishing particular goals and tasks as well as explaining when and why the skills should be used.

The *attitude* objectives refer to the intrapersonal domain, including attributes such as flexibility, motivation, appreciation for diversity, metacognition, perseverance, attribution of failure and success in learning, and self-efficacy. Read any list of 21st century standards, and you will find references to the development of competencies and skills in the affective domain, including collaboration, initiative, involvement, responsibility, and task orientation, to name a few (McMillan, 2011).

It is abundantly clear that with the increasing emphasis on developing 21st century skills, there is a need for integrating knowledge, skills, and attitudes in instruction so students can grow holistically (Baartman & de Bruijn, 2011). Thus, when planning for learning objectives, all three areas should be thoughtfully addressed.

As an illustration, following are sample daily objectives developed by Holly Wrighson, the fifth-grade social studies teacher whose unit plan on the Roman Republic was featured in chapter 1. Following are the specific learning objectives of that student project. These learning objectives not only target students' mastery of the content about the Roman Republic but also the development of skills in cooperative learning (H. Wrighson, personal communication, March 6, 2014).

What does your teacher want you to learn?

1. Learn how Romans designed and built capital cities in the provinces they ruled.

2. Learn how teamwork improves projects.

How will you know you have learned it?

1. In small groups, you will design a Roman provincial city complete with all the elements of Roman life.

2. Team reflections show growth in cooperation, negotiation, and organization skills.

These learning objectives explain the expected learning in student-friendly and developmentally appropriate language. They are also learner-centered and succinctly describe the performance that students should be able to demonstrate after the learning experience. Wrighson reflects on these learning objectives as follows.

> I establish objectives and outcomes during the initial phase of new learning and use them to guide the instructional and assessment process. I always identify what knowledge and skills I want students to develop before we start a new learning unit. This set of learning objectives is succinct, but it shows that my instruction not only requires recall of factual information but also develops higher-level learning ability and social skills. I also create a rubric to go with the general objectives. The rubric includes a representative sample of performance terms to clarify for students what is acceptable as evidence for attaining the objectives. (H. Wrighson, personal communication, March 6, 2014)

The following is another example of learning objectives, this time written by fifth-grade English teacher, Lana Czeski. In this lesson, students elaborate on a memory of a place they visited using the five senses (see, hear, taste, smell, and feel) to work on increasing their word choice in writing. Czeski explains the rationale for this learning, stating that writing is more interesting to read if the writer is aware of his or her elaboration on a topic through specific word choice (L. Czeski, personal communication, March 4, 2014).

> Learning Objectives
>
> - I can write an informative piece explaining a topic using an introduction, related facts, details, and a concluding statement.
> - I can write narratives to develop real experiences or events using dialogue, descriptive details, transitional words, and a logical conclusion.
> - I can write to develop my ideas in a clear and organized way.
> - I can work with others to produce writing.
> - I can have 50 percent of my homework by Monday with 85 percent accuracy in answers.

Czeski reflects on these learning objectives as follows.

> It is important that students are able to articulate the learning expectations and feel like they can achieve success. Therefore, I write objectives using 'I can' language in terms

students can understand. Communicating and displaying objectives on a daily basis not only focuses students' attention on the learning, but also helps them master the learning. (L. Czeski, personal communication, March 4, 2014)

Aligning Objectives, Instructional Strategies, and Assessment

Designing learning objectives also involves clearly delineating the instructional model of how learning is expected to develop and how assessments measure student progress toward attaining the objectives. Learning objectives should be communicated explicitly to students and used continuously and seamlessly to monitor student learning and provide feedback regarding progress (Reed, 2012). Figure 2.2 shows the relationship between learning objectives, instruction and learning activities, and assessments. Learning experiences are optimal when these three components are congruent with one another.

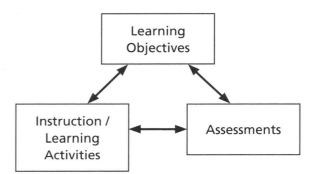

Figure 2.2: Aligning objectives, instruction and learning activities, and assessment.

Summary

Learning objectives are brief statements that describe what students are expected to learn by the end of a unit, lesson, or project. They are interim steps that propel students to work toward more comprehensive learning standards. In this chapter, we discussed how to develop learning objectives using the cognitive taxonomy, how to create trifold objectives that cover the full range of learning outcomes, and the importance of aligning objectives, classroom activities, and assessment.

To close, we provide several handouts to help teachers in their journey toward developing effective learning objectives.

The terms *goals* and *objectives* sometimes are used interchangeably, while in other circumstances, teachers draw a distinction between them. Typically, goals are broader and focus on the big picture and long-term evaluations, and sometimes, they are not directly measurable. In comparison, objectives are more specific and measurable. The handout "Steps for Writing Learning Objectives" (page 28) draws on the framework established by the seminal work of Robert Mager (1997) to guide teachers in developing solid learning objectives.

Effective teachers develop quality (thoughtful, accurate, and meaningful) learning objectives to promote deeper learning competencies with their students. The handout "Learning Objectives Assessment Rubric" (page 29) provides guidelines to assess whether objectives focus on quality learning experiences.

The imperative to develop 21st century skills and deeper learning has significant implications for teachers in terms of what to teach and how to teach. The new paradigms of thinking about how to prepare students for college and careers also influence teachers' practices of generating goals and objectives. The handout "Trifold Objectives: Knowledge and Skills" (page 30) provides a template (with prompts excerpted from the Hewlett Foundation's deeper learning competencies) to help teachers identify the knowledge and skills that goals and objectives should target, either by lesson, unit, semester, or year (Ark & Schneider, 2014; Huberman, Bitter, Anthony, & O'Day, 2014).

Noncognitive skills are important predictors of students' academic success and future workplace outcomes. These skills should be developed in the classroom. The handout "Trifold Objectives: Dispositions (Noncognitive)" (page 32) offers prompts (excerpted from the Hewlett Foundation's deeper learning competencies) that help teachers to identify appropriate noncognitive objectives (Ark & Schneider, 2014; Huberman et al., 2014).

Steps for Writing Learning Objectives

Instructions: Learning objectives should satisfy the following criteria. Circle *Yes* or *No* to indicate if each criterion has been met.

1. Objectives are stated in terms of expected student performance (not teacher performance).

    Yes   No

2. Objectives contain specific, action-oriented, measurable verbs, such as *identify, list, explain, name, describe, demonstrate,* and *compare,* rather than verbs that cannot be observed and measured, such as *learn, know, understand,* and *appreciate.*

    Yes   No

3. Objectives specify the condition under which the students are expected to perform.

    Yes   No

4. Objectives specify the criteria to use to determine whether the performance is acceptable.

    Yes   No

Behavior	The behavior should be specific and observable.
Condition	The condition refers to under which circumstance the behavior is to be completed, including what tools or assistance are provided.
Standard	The standard refers to the criterion of expected performance, such as the accuracy rate.

Incorrect: Students will understand and recognize literacy devices.

Correct:

          Condition   **Behavior**   **Standard**

            ↓   ↓   ↓

By completing the activities, students will be able to *recognize and list at least six literary devices found in Act I of* Romeo and Juliet.

Incorrect: Students will understand the processes of reasoning.

Correct:

                                          Condition   **Behavior**

                                           ↓   ↓

Students will read two letters from the editorial page of a newspaper or magazine. They will be able to select, evaluate, and discuss the type of logic employed, the effectiveness of the evidence, and the validity for at least five arguments in the reading materials. The ratings used should be no lower than 15 (out of 20) points based on the evaluation rubrics.

                                                                     ↑

                                                                   Standard

Now, examine your learning objectives, and see if they capture the three criteria listed above. If they do not, please try to revise them.

Source: Adapted from Mager, R. F. (1997). Preparing instructional objectives: A critical tool in the development of effective instruction (3rd ed.). Atlanta, GA: Center for Effective Performance.

Learning Objectives Assessment Rubric

	Strongly Disagree	Disagree	Agree	Strongly Agree
The objectives contain compelling subject content.				
The objectives help students frame specific questions.				
The objectives imply that high-quality products must be produced by students.				
The objectives will be judged with standards-based rubrics.				
The objectives contribute to long-term, accumulative learning.				
The objectives build in milestones to keep learning on track.				
The objectives guide the delivery of instruction and evaluation of student learning.				
The objectives help students focus on and set priorities.				
The objectives make teaching more organized.				
The objectives guide student self-assessment.				
The objectives are congruent with the learning activities.				
The objectives are congruent with the assessment.				
The objectives incorporate student learning and development in subject knowledge, skills, and attitudes.				
The objectives focus on higher-order thinking (such as application, analysis, creativity, and evaluation in Bloom's taxonomy).				
The objectives are realistic and achievable.				
The objectives are consistent with the goals of the curriculum.				
The objectives are clearly stated.				

Trifold Objectives: Knowledge and Skills

Knowledge Objectives

Competencies	Definitions	Prompts	How will your learning objectives cover these competencies?
Mastery of core content knowledge	Students develop and draw from a baseline understanding of knowledge in an academic discipline and are able to transfer knowledge to other situations.	• Students understand key principles and relationships within a content area and organize information in a conceptual framework. • Students learn, remember, and recall facts relevant to a content area. • Students have procedural knowledge of a content area and know how content knowledge is produced and how experts solve problems. • Students know and are able to use the language specific to a content area. • Students extend core knowledge to novel tasks and situations in a variety of academic subjects. • Students learn and can apply theories relevant to a content area. • Students apply facts, processes, and theories to real-world situations.	

page 1 of 2

Skills Objectives

Competencies	Definitions	Prompts	How will your learning objectives cover these competencies?
Critical thinking and solving complex problems	Students apply tools and techniques gleaned from core subjects to formulate and solve problems. These tools include data analysis, statistical reasoning, scientific inquiry, creative problem solving, nonlinear thinking, and persistence.	• Students are familiar with and effectively use the tools and techniques specific to a content area. • Students formulate problems and generate hypotheses. • Students identify data and information needed to solve a problem. • Students apply tools and techniques specific to a content area to gather necessary data and information. • Students evaluate, integrate, and critically analyze multiple sources of information. • Students monitor and refine the problem-solving process, as needed, based on available data. • Students reason and construct justifiable arguments in support of a hypothesis. • Students persist to solve complex problems.	

Sources: Adapted from Ark, T. V., & Schneider, C. (2014). Deeper learning for every student every day. *Menlo Park, CA: Hewlett Foundation. Accessed at www.hewlett.org/sites/default/files/Deeper%20Learning%20for%20Every%20Student%20EVery%20Day _GETTING%20SMART_1.2014.pdf on April 30, 2015; Huberman, M., Bitter, C., Anthony, J., & O'Day, J. (2014, September).* The shape of deeper learning: Strategies, structures, and cultures in deeper learning network high schools. *Washington, DC: American Institutes for Research.*

Trifold Objectives: Dispositions (Noncognitive)

Competencies	Definitions	Prompts	How will your learning objectives cover these competencies?
Collaboration (interpersonal)	Students cooperate to identify and create solutions to academic, social, vocational, and personal challenges.	• Students collaborate with others to complete tasks and solve problems successfully. • Students work as part of a group to identify group goals. • Students participate in a team to plan problem-solving steps and identify resources necessary to meet group goals. • Students communicate and incorporate multiple points of view to meet group goals.	
Communication (interpersonal)	Students clearly organize their data, findings, and thoughts in both written and oral communication.	• Students communicate complex concepts to others in both written and oral presentations. • Students structure information and data in meaningful and useful ways. • Students listen to and incorporate feedback and ideas from others. • Students provide constructive and appropriate feedback to their peers. • Students understand that creating a quality final communication requires review and revision of multiple drafts. • Students tailor their message for the intended audience.	

Competencies	Definitions	Prompts	How will your learning objectives cover these competencies?
Learning-to-learn competencies (intrapersonal)	Students monitor and direct their own learning.	• Students set a goal for each learning task, monitor their progress toward the goal, and adapt their approach as needed to successfully complete a task or solve a problem. • Students know and can apply a variety of study skills and strategies to meet the demands of a task. • Students monitor their comprehension as they learn, recognize when they become confused or encounter obstacles, diagnose barriers to their success, and select appropriate strategies to work through them. • Students work well independently but ask for help when needed. • Students routinely reflect on their learning experiences and apply insights to subsequent situations. • Students are aware of their strengths and weaknesses and anticipate needing to work harder in some areas. • Students identify and work toward lifelong learning and academic goals. • Students enjoy and seek out learning on their own and with others. • Students anticipate and are prepared to meet changing expectations in a variety of academic, professional, and social environments. • Students delay gratification, refocus after distractions, and maintain momentum until they reach their goals. • Students use failures and setbacks as opportunities for feedback and apply lessons learned to improve future efforts. • Students care about the quality of their work and put in extra effort to do things thoroughly and well. • Students continue looking for new ways to learn challenging material or solve difficult problems.	

Instructional Planning for Effective Teaching © 2016 Solution Tree Press • solution-tree.com
Visit **go.solution-tree.com/instruction** to download this page.

Competencies	Definitions	Prompts	How will your learning objectives cover these competencies?
Developing academic mindsets (intrapersonal)	Students develop positive attitudes and beliefs about themselves as learners that increase their academic perseverance and prompt them to engage in productive academic behaviors. Students are committed to seeing work through to completion, meeting their goals and doing quality work, and searching for solutions to overcome obstacles.	• Students feel a strong sense of belonging within a community of learners and value intellectual engagement with others. • Students understand learning as a social process and actively learn from one another and support each other in pursuit of learning goals. • Students readily engage in the construction of meaning and understanding through interaction with peers. • Students trust in their own capacity and competence and feel a strong sense of efficacy in a variety of academic tasks. • Students see themselves as academic achievers and expect to succeed in their learning pursuits. • Students believe that hard work will pay off in increased knowledge and skills. • Students are motivated to put in the time and effort needed to build a solid knowledge base and to accomplish important goals. • Students perceive the inherent value of content knowledge, learning, and developing skills. • Students see the relevance of schoolwork to their lives and interests. • Students understand how work they do now will benefit them in the future. • Students know that future learning will build on what they know and learn today.	

Sources: Adapted from Ark, T. V., & Schneider, C. (2014). Deeper learning for every student every day. *Menlo Park, CA: Hewlett Foundation. Accessed at www.hewlett.org/sites/default/files/Deeper%20Learning%20for%20Every%20Student%20EVery%20Day _GETTING%20SMART_1.2014.pdf on April 30, 2015; Huberman, M., Bitter, C., Anthony, J., & O'Day, J. (2014, September).* The shape of deeper learning: Strategies, structures, and cultures in deeper learning network high schools. *Washington, DC: American Institutes for Research.*

Chapter 3
Organizing Learning Activities

The best teachers never walk into the classroom with a blank slate. Indeed, organization is a hallmark of good teaching. Fluidity, flexibility, and teachable moments are all important. But without structure and organization, there is no instructional plan. As early as 1976, Hartley and Davies stated:

> The sequencing and arrangement of subject material appears to influence not only what students learn, but also their attitudes towards the usefulness and importance of what has to be achieved. For this reason, any procedure which makes this arrangement or organization more obvious and striking is likely to facilitate the learning of meaningful material. Nowhere is this more important than in the preliminary phases of teaching and instruction. (p. 239)

As suggested in this quote, organizing learning activities is an essential aspect of effective instructional planning. When teachers design learning activities, they must consider how to orchestrate the actions in their classrooms to support the strategies they have chosen. Consequently, the quality of learning—even the opportunity to learn—depends on substantial prearranging and preparing of materials, planning for activity structure, and skillful managing of workflow (LePage, Darling-Hammond, & Akar, 2005). In fact, when teachers consider the organizational aspects of their lessons, the instruction is more effective and efficient.

What Research Says About Organizing Learning Activities

Research shows that it is important to organize instruction logically both at a macro level—ranging across a number of lessons; and at a micro level—within each specific class period. This section examines the advantages of both macro-level planning and micro-level planning.

Big-Picture Planning and Organizing

Research finds that effective teachers carefully plan activities that have clear goals and a logical structure with a step-by-step content progression (Zahorik et al., 2003). The best learning objectives are worthless if they are not properly implemented—therefore, "the skillful orchestration of the objectives, strategies, materials, and equipment and the careful organization, development, and sequencing of the lesson are absolutely crucial to successful teaching" (Lambert, 1988, p. 54). Studies indicate that student learning is associated with the amount, depth, and coherence of content coverage a teacher accomplishes (Plewis, 1998; Shield & Dole, 2013; Stols, 2013). These studies point to the importance of deliberately organizing instruction so that it optimizes the subject content to be covered.

A study examining 261 lesson plans from 39 teachers in urban, low-performing middle schools in New England find that lesson coherence in design is important in determining the effectiveness of planning (Panasuk & Todd, 2005). Carefully organizing a lesson or instructional unit involves not only thoughtful preparation of specific lessons or units but also long-term planning to ensure coverage of the curriculum. Sequencing is an important aspect of logically structuring lessons. Karrie Jones, Jennifer Jones, and Paul Vermette (2011) find that less effective teachers typically do not show evidence of idea development in their lesson planning. A lack of sequential planning leads to teaching concepts to students in isolation, which requires students to try to connect ideas and form understanding on their own. Students may then develop misconceptions and misunderstandings about how concepts relate.

Small-Picture Planning and Organizing

In addition to ensuring that multiple lessons (or instructional units) are sequenced appropriately, it is essential that individual lesson components are sequenced appropriately. This provides order and familiarity for students so they know what to expect during the lesson. Having a sequential lesson also ensures that all aspects of the lesson are covered and in order.

In an early study, Jacob Kounin (1977, as cited in LePage et al., 2005) videotaped eighty classrooms defined as either orderly or disorderly. In the analysis of teachers' organizational behaviors, he observes that selected actions by a teacher could hinder the momentum and smoothness of a lesson—for example, when a teacher terminates one activity, starts another, and then returns to the first activity, it disrupts the flow. Teachers also disrupt the flow when they move away from an activity for unimportant matters or when they slow down instruction by explaining directions in detail when students already understand. Thus, smooth organization and structure—from the planning process and carried right through instructional delivery—are essential to good planning.

How to Move From Research to Practice

It is essential for the instructional planning process to be organized. Within that organization, there must be alignment in all aspects, particularly the learning objectives, activities, and assessment. This applies to both big-picture and small-picture planning.

Steps for Organizing Instruction

Some helpful strategies for organizing instruction include the following (Estes, Mintz, & Gunter, 2010).

- Analyze the content forms.
- Order the content.
- Plan the scope and depth.
- Plan the sequence.

Analyze the Content Forms

Divide the learning content into major categories: facts, concepts, and processes. These three categories make up a large part of the instructional content. Select the most meaningful combinations in the design process.

Order the Content

New learning is built on prior knowledge. Be sure to anchor new learning on what students already know. Move from simple to complex. Any stage of learning and understanding builds on a previous, more general level. A concept can be presented at many different levels of generality and complexity. It typically is easier to understand the higher, more general level and harder to understand the more refined, specialized level.

Plan the Scope and Depth

Consider the following questions when deciding the scope and depth of a given curriculum.

- What are the important knowledge, concepts, skills, and attitudes for students to master?
- Given the parameters of time and developmental readiness, to what broad areas of study should students be exposed?
- How broadly should various skills and concepts be presented?
- How much time is needed to engage in various learning activities at an appropriate depth?

Plan the Sequence

Consider the following questions when deciding the sequence of learning.

- At what stage are students ready for certain curriculum experiences?
- What developmental transitions are appropriate in shaping curricular order?
- Should subjects be ordered chronologically or thematically? In subjects such as mathematics, a hierarchy of knowledge is already well established. The sequence of learning is usually prescribed in a linear fashion. However, in subjects such as social studies, there is no agreed-on hierarchy of knowledge. The sequence of learning is usually established by interest, themes, or variety.

The sample lesson plan in figure 3.1 illustrates how activities and actions in a lesson can be organized in a coherent fashion.

Standard

Interpret a multiplication equation as a comparison (for example, interpret 35 = 5 x 7 as a statement that 35 is 5 times as many as 7 and 7 times as many as 5). Represent verbal statements of multiplicative comparison as multiplication equations.

Materials

Interactive whiteboard, document camera, 12-sided die, 6-sided die, 1-cm grid paper, ½-inch grid paper, colored pencils or crayons, whiteboard and marker, notebook paper, pencil

Anticipatory Set

Working in pairs, students demonstrate previous knowledge of multiplication arrays by using dice to roll a number and color the array on grid paper. Play alternates until one player's multiplication array cannot fit on the grid paper. Higher-level students use a 12-sided die and 1-cm grid paper. Lower-level students use a 6-sided die and ½-inch grid paper.

Students use two different colors to differentiate their arrays. When play cannot continue, each student adds up the area of his or her array to determine who has the higher sum. Give a ten-minute time limit for this activity.

Objective

By the end of the lesson, students will be able to correctly:

- Create word problems that correspond to given multiplication equations
- Create multiplication equations that correspond to given word problems

Purpose

The lesson will:

- Increase students' understanding of multiplication
- Increase students' understanding of the commutative property of multiplication
- Show students the connection between equations and problems

Input

- Discuss with students the vocabulary related to arrays, multiplication equations, and multiplication properties (commutative).
- With students, create a circle map of words related to multiplication.
- Review the parts of an equation.

Model

- Show students how to correctly use the number rolled on the dice to create an array on grid paper.
- Show students how to write a question that corresponds to a given multiplication equation.
- Show students how to write an equation that corresponds to a multiplication word problem.

Check for Understanding

- Have students create multiplication arrays on grid paper.
- Have students create word problems from equations.
- Have students create equations from word problems.

Guided Practice

- Have students work in small groups to allow for discussion and collaboration.
- Continue to guide students as they work individually on their assignments. Invite them to raise their hands if they need help.

Figure 3.1: Sample lesson plan—Fourth-grade mathematics.   continued ⟶

Closure

- Ask students to list multiplication key words on their whiteboards.
- Have students write a multiplication equation on their whiteboards that represents a given question.

Independent Practice

- Have students create two word problems that correspond to two given equations.
- Have students create three multiplication equations that correspond to three given word problems.

Accommodations

- Gifted: Give students a 12-sided die for arrays. Ask them to use a variety of variables in their equations. Give students grid paper to create arrays based on their independent practice problems.
- Learning resource: Give students a 6-sided die for arrays. Ask them to create one word problem and two multiplication equations with the complexity matched to their individual performance level.

Source: James H. Stronge. Used with permission.

Theoretical Frameworks for Organizing Instruction

Many prominent theoretical frameworks have been introduced regarding instructional design. From these frameworks emerged various approaches to creating and organizing learning experiences. The following section highlights a few such approaches: inductive versus deductive, advance organizers, and sequencing.

Inductive Versus Deductive

One helpful strategy for organizing instruction at the lesson level is to consider using an inductive versus deductive approach. For inductive organization, teachers give students specific data, examples, or facts. Through the process of investigation and reasoning, students form the generalization, rule, or concept definition. This process moves from specific to general.

For deductive organization, the instruction leans toward being direct. Teachers begin the lesson by presenting a main idea, generalization, conclusion, rule, or concept definition. They then give students specific examples, rationales, and clarifications. This process moves from general to specific.

Advance Organizers

Another helpful way to organize lessons is to develop advance organizers. Advance organizers are more than overviews of new content; they specifically illustrate the relationship and bridge the gap between students' prior learning and new learning. David Ausubel distinguishes two kinds of advance organizers: comparative and expository (as cited in Dell'Olio & Donk, 2007).

Comparative organizers are used when the knowledge to be acquired is relatively familiar to students. These organizers activate students' prior learning, integrate new learning with prior learning, and discriminate between new and existing learning.

Expository organizers are used when new learning material is unfamiliar to students. The purpose of expository organizers is to provide learners with a conceptual framework for unfamiliar content and concepts.

In applying advance organizers, familiarity with new materials is key to determining which type should be used.

Sequencing

A key aspect of organizing instruction is *sequencing*, which can be defined as developing a logical plan for instructional activities that helps students effectively master knowledge or skills in an organized way. Presenting knowledge in a series of carefully interrelated steps not only helps students master content but also develops skills in making connections across components of the unit or overall curriculum (Orlich, Harder, Callahan, Trevisan, & Brown, 2009).

According to Donald Orlich et al. (2009), sequencing has two basic purposes.

1. To isolate an aspect of a given knowledge base (for example, a fact, concept, generalization, or principle) so students understand its unique characteristics—a function that helps make learning more manageable

2. To relate the knowledge or process being taught to a larger organized body of knowledge—a function that makes learning more meaningful

Allan Ornstein and Thomas Lasley (2004) note two different views for lesson sequencing, depending on the instructional approach—transmission or constructivist.

The transmission approach can be used when the teacher's goal is to teach discrete processes; it follows a typical sequence of explanations and lectures, demonstrations and modeling, questioning to check for understanding, and practice and drill. In the first step, explanations and lectures, it is important to follow a planned sequence that minimizes diversions or tangential discussions (Ornstein & Lasley, 2004). In addition, explanations of concepts should be included in the proper place to maintain the sequence of knowledge building discussed previously. In an older yet still highly relevant set of guidelines, Barak Rosenshine (1986) states that when effective teachers teach concepts and skills explicitly, they do the following.

- Begin a lesson with a short statement of goals

- Begin a lesson with a short review of previous, prerequisite learning

- Present new material in small steps, with student practice after each step

- Give clear, detailed instructions and explanations

- Provide active practice for all students

- Ask many questions, check for student understanding, and obtain responses from all students

- Guide students during initial practice

- Provide systematic feedback and corrections

- Provide explicit instruction and practice for seatwork exercises and, when necessary, monitor students during seatwork

- Continue practice until students are independent and confident. (pp. 61–62)

Similarly, John Zahorik et al. (2003) find that "more effective teachers' primary teaching method was explicit, step-by-step instruction" (p. 76). This allows the teacher to give clear directions, explain concepts in a logical manner, model the concepts, provide feedback, and adapt the information as necessary.

The constructivist approach to instructional sequencing can be used when students cocreate with teacher involvement and guidance. The nature of this type of lesson requires a different sequence for lesson presentation. The constructivist view, according to Ornstein and Lasley (2004), must follow this step-by-step process.

1. Present new information within the context of prior knowledge and previous learning.

2. Assign students active, hands-on tasks that require them to explore, analyze, solve problems, and form their own explanations.

3. Allow students to use multiple ways to demonstrate learning.

4. Provide ways for students to engage in metacognitive learning—to think about how they think.

While the constructivist approach differs from the transmission approach in purpose and sequence, the sequence of building knowledge from a base is the same. When designing the sequence of learning activities, the most effective teachers know when to teach from a transmission view and when to teach from a constructivist view.

Summary

In this chapter, we explored how the order and organization of learning activities can affect the scope and depth of curriculum coverage as well as the way information is processed and retained. We also examined how different learning theories can influence the sequence of instructional and learning experiences. During the planning process, teachers must consider both learning goals and students' learning needs in order to determine the sequence and organization of instruction.

To close, we provide several handouts to help teachers in their journey toward planning well-designed and organized instruction.

Having a well-organized, bird's-eye view of instruction and learning gives both teachers and students a useful perspective of what lies ahead (Hartley & Davies, 1976). The inductive and deductive approaches are two potential ways to organize learning activities in a lesson. The handout "Organizing Instruction" (page 41) provides a tool to help teachers think about the lessons in their subject area in which these two forms of organization might apply.

In designing learning experiences, teachers must choose the best way to prepare students for and introduce them to new and unfamiliar situations and knowledge. This is usually accomplished by means of some kind of introductory strategy, such as advance organizers, which serve as a framework in which subsequent learning can be arranged and related. Teachers also can use the "Organizing Instruction" handout to make the connection between what students already know and what they are about to learn with the use of advance organizers. They might consider in what cases the two types of advance organizers work best in their classrooms.

The handout "Organizing Instruction: Self-Assessment" (page 42) captures major ideas that can be used by teachers to either guide or assess the process of organizing learning activities. These ideas can help teachers examine their practices of organizing instruction at a more refined and nuanced level. Education leaders may adapt the handout to assess teachers' performance in this area and to guide feedback. They also can use it to scaffold conversations with teachers on improving planning for instructional design.

Classroom organization is an integral component of organizing instruction, as seating, work areas, and student movement can either facilitate or impede learning. Therefore, planning for classroom organization should be part of the overall planning process and happen *before* students arrive. Conceptualizing a plan for organizing the classroom, including seating arrangements for various learning activities, makes the implementation of learning activities more effective and efficient. The handout "Organizing Your Classroom" (page 43) provides a number of elements that teachers should consider in planning for physical classroom organization. It also aims to ensure the alignment between classroom organization and learning activities.

Organizing Instruction

Inductive Versus Deductive

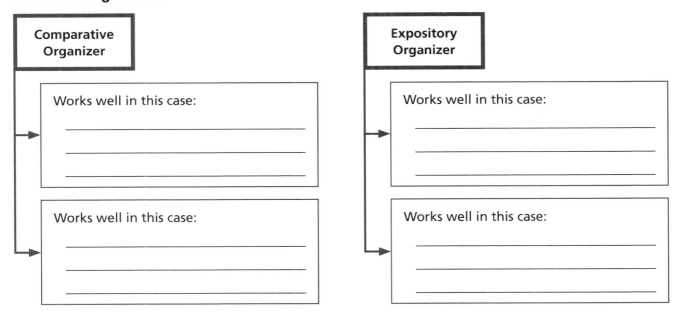

Inductive Organization

Works well in this case:

_____

_____

_____

Works well in this case:

_____

_____

_____

Deductive Organization

Works well in this case:

_____

_____

_____

Works well in this case:

_____

_____

_____

Advance Organizers

Comparative Organizer

Works well in this case:

_____

_____

_____

Works well in this case:

_____

_____

_____

Expository Organizer

Works well in this case:

_____

_____

_____

Works well in this case:

_____

_____

_____

Source: Adapted from Ausubel, D. (1978). In defense of advance organizers: A reply to the critics. Review of Educational Research, 48(2), 251–257.

Organizing Instruction: Self-Assessment

	Poor ←——→ Excellent				
	1	2	3	4	5
The central focus of classroom time is on teaching and learning.					
The time allocated for each segment of learning is logical and defensible.					
Lesson organization includes a component for introductory activities that prepare students for the day's learning and relate new learning to their prior knowledge.					
Learning activities are logically sequenced and are able to maintain momentum within the lesson.					
The physical organization of the classroom is optimal for the successful implementation of learning activities.					
Student behavioral expectations are established and communicated to minimize disruption and maximize engagement time.					
The transition between learning activities is smooth and efficient.					
The learning activities are structured around key concepts, terms, and skills to be learned.					
Lesson organization ensures that key understanding is established prior to moving on (for example, using quick assessment probes).					
Lesson organization allows flexibility in pacing to accommodate necessary changes based on student understanding.					
Lesson organization allows for opportunities to reinforce prior learning and contribute to cumulative (long-term) learning goals.					
The overall learning experience comes together as a dynamic whole, which allows students to integrate new ideas with preexisting ones.					

Instructional Planning for Effective Teaching © 2016 J. H. Stronge • solution-tree.com

Visit **go.solution-tree.com/instruction** to download this page.

Organizing Your Classroom

Learning Activity 1:	Learning Activity 2:	Learning Activity 3:	Learning Activity 4:
Purpose:	Purpose:	Purpose:	Purpose:
Student Seating Arrangement:	Student Seating Arrangement:	Student Seating Arrangement:	Student Seating Arrangement:
Students' Role:	Students' Role:	Students' Role:	Students' Role:
Teacher Seating:	Teacher Seating:	Teacher Seating:	Teacher Seating:
Teacher's Role:	Teacher's Role:	Teacher's Role:	Teacher's Role:
Materials/Resources:	Materials/Resources:	Materials/Resources:	Materials/Resources:
Procedures:	Procedures:	Procedures:	Procedures:
Rules and Expectations:	Rules and Expectations:	Rules and Expectations:	Rules and Expectations:
Assessment:	Assessment:	Assessment:	Assessment:

Chapter 4

Selecting Meaningful and Purposeful Learning Materials

Some teachers might mistakenly believe that learning is a mechanical process—one in which information is transferred from textbooks to students, and students acquire knowledge and skills through listening, reading, and memorization. The reality is that teaching and learning are far more complex. The way learners interact with new information is influenced by their experiences, prior knowledge, and beliefs, and they often fail to remember, understand, and apply new information that has no connection or context for acquiring meaning (Hammerness, Darling-Hammond, & Bransford, 2005).

Effective teachers understand that instructional planning must be tied to the core curricula and teachers' instructional strategies, not dictated by materials and equipment. Instructional materials, including textbooks, serve a supportive rather than central role in the connection between curriculum and instruction. Effective teaching is much more than acting out scripts written by textbook and test publishers. Textbooks—that is, good textbooks—can serve as an indispensable resource to teachers; however, allowing textbooks to dominate instructional planning is unlikely to meet today's educational demands for real-world critical thinking, problem solving, skill building, and inquiry. Furthermore, many contemporary topics are too specific and others are too new to be included in textbooks (Sharma & Elbow, 2000).

Despite these limitations, teachers must be well-informed and resourceful in considering and selecting quality instructional materials in their efforts to improve student learning. To prepare students for the world beyond the classroom, teachers need to "develop ways for them to learn from information, as they will encounter it in real-life situations, information that is not predigested, carefully selected, or logically organized" (Stripling, 1999, p. 6). Consequently, good teachers understand the necessity of incorporating into the design of their instructional plans *meaningful and purposeful learning materials*.

What Research Says About Meaningful and Purposeful Learning Materials

Research finds that one key characteristic of effective teachers is that they evaluate resources to use when planning a unit or lesson. They use criteria such as grade-level appropriateness, curriculum standard alignment, information accuracy, time available to teach, and learning benefits. They also enhance the instructional benefits of resources by minimizing time allocated to less relevant or unnecessary material (Buttram & Waters, 1997).

One study uses multiple regression analyses to identify the effectiveness of individual teachers by measuring their ability to improve student academic achievement (Haynie, 2006). Through examining the instructional practices of the ten most effective and ten least effective biology teachers in a given school district, the researcher finds that the top teachers reach beyond prepared resources to plan their own activities, while most low-performing teachers use prepared resources. Top teachers also use student assessment data to plan instruction. Based on data drawn from frequent assessments, they make data-driven decisions about what goals and objectives to address and what learning materials to select. Thus, there is a logical and direct connection running from curriculum to instructional strategies to instructional materials in their planning.

Richard Allington and Peter Johnston (2000) also find that the instruction of effective teachers is multisourced in terms of material selection. Exemplary teachers are inclined to stretch the reading and writing learning experiences beyond the textbooks. For instance, while planning for a lesson in social science, effective teachers usually use historical fiction, biography, Internet and magazine resources, and other content sources.

Cheryl Torrez and Scott Waring (2009) examine students' experiences in learning to use primary sources in historical inquiry. In the study, two teacher educators develop and teach social studies lessons in collaboration with fifth- and sixth-grade teachers. The students in these classes have little previous experience evaluating primary sources and artifacts. Using both digital and nondigital primary sources, the students begin to understand historical perspective and use historical evidence as the basis of their conclusions. At the end of this study, teachers indicate that their students are more engaged in social studies. Drawing from these and similar studies, it seems safe to say that effective teachers improve student learning through enriched instructional materials.

How to Move From Research to Practice

Finding and selecting the appropriate learning materials is an essential component of instructional planning. While there are many vital facets to designing, adapting, or adopting instructional materials, three of particular note stand out: (1) authenticity of materials, (2) appropriateness to students' developmental levels and learning readiness, and (3) adapting online resources for classroom use.

Authentic Learning Materials

Students are not empty vessels that need to be filled with knowledge but rather active learners who are able to construct their own knowledge and form their own theories. Students learn best when they are interacting with and completing authentic and meaningful work. An essential aspect of effective instruction that helps build and sustain authenticity and student engagement

is relevance of the instruction. In fact, making instruction relevant to real-world problems is among the most powerful instructional practices a teacher can use to increase student learning (Schroeder, Scott, Tolson, Huang, & Lee, 2007; Wenglinsky, 2004).

Authentic learning is defined as a "wide variety of educational and instructional techniques focused on connecting what students are taught in school to real-world issues, problems, and applications" (Glossary of Education Reform, 2013a).

Relevance is defined as the "learning experiences that are either directly applicable to the personal aspirations, interests, or cultural experiences of students (personal relevance) or that are connected in some way to real-world issues, problems, and contexts (life relevance)" (Glossary of Education Reform, 2013b).

Authentic and relevant learning allows students to explore, inquire, and meaningfully construct knowledge of real problems that are relevant to their lives. Moreover, students are motivated and engaged when the focus of instruction is on meaningful conceptualization, especially when the learning process and the outcomes have authentic bearing on students' lives. Learners appreciate the learning task when their own knowledge of the world is valued. For example, instead of teaching students about imperialism and colonialism, teachers might invite students of different cultural backgrounds to work on a project exploring the effects of Imperialism and Colonialism from the perspective of their racial or cultural heritage. Consider the following two examples shown in figure 4.1 for transforming teacher-centered learning targets into profound and meaningful student-centered learning experiences (Wiggins, 2010).

Furthermore, authentic learning experiences should incorporate the following nine principles, which ultimately impact materials development and selection for the most beneficial instruction (Authentic Learning, n.d.; Herrington, Reeves, & Oliver, 2010).

1. Authentic contexts that reflect the way the knowledge is used in real life

2. Authentic tasks and activities that are relevant to students' lives

3. Access to expert performance and process modeling

4. Multiple roles and perspectives

5. Collaborative construction of knowledge

6. Reflection to think about and discuss choices

7. Articulation so that tacit knowledge is explicit

8. Coaching and scaffolding at critical times

9. Authentic assessment of learning

Example 1

Teacher centered: My goal is to teach students about the U.S. Constitution and the three branches of government.

Student centered: My goal is to teach you about the three branches of government so you become an informed and committed citizen, aware that our government was built to counter human flaws and fallibility and be responsive to citizen feedback.

Example 2

Teacher centered: My goal is to teach students how to graph linear relationships.

Student centered: My goal is to teach you to make sense of linear relationships so you will be able to solve problems with linear and non-linear relationships and recognize on your own which kind of relationship it is.

Source: Adapted from Wiggins, 2010.

Figure 4.1: Examples of teacher-centered versus student-centered learning targets.

Developmentally Appropriate Learning Materials

Learning materials, no matter how well they are organized and how appealing they may be, won't contribute significantly to learning outcomes unless they are congruent with students' development level and learning readiness. Relevant to the idea of appropriateness is Jean Piaget's (1997) concept of adaptation, referring to what happens when new knowledge is acquired. Two major processes occur as children make sense of their world: assimilation and accommodation. They either assimilate new information in relation to prior knowledge and understanding, or they modify existing knowledge to accommodate new insights. In other words, *new knowledge should have a strong connection with prior learning*.

Appropriateness is also relevant to Lev Vygotsky's zone of proximal development. According to Vygotsky (1978), the zone of proximal development is "the distance between the actual developmental level as determined by individual problem solving and the level of potential development as determined through problem solving under adult guidance or in collaboration with more capable peers" (p. 86). Applying this idea to instructional planning implies that the teacher must be knowledgeable of students' current capabilities and be able to select and design learning materials that are challenging (the new learning is beyond students' current knowledge and cannot be accomplished alone) but reachable with the teacher's assistance. Simply stated, the materials should be developmentally appropriate.

Developmentally appropriate practice is discussed mostly in the field of early childhood education; however, the concept and practice are essential to instruction for learners of any age. In selecting and designing learning materials and learning experiences, teachers should have sound knowledge of child development and learning processes to cater to students' needs, particularly in the areas of emotional, social, cognitive, and metacognitive development.

Online Resources

The Internet increasingly is used as the supplemental and, in some cases, primary source of information for teaching and learning. In this information-rich era, vast quantities of both commercial and free learning materials are available to choose from. To illustrate, query a search engine on any given instructional topic and the likely result will be overwhelming. You will find books, pamphlets, reports, maps, posters, videos, how-to guides, lesson plans, and so on. Many of these options are well-designed and properly vetted materials published or prepared by reputable and conscientious organizations or individuals; others are useless.

So, how does a teacher sort out the treasures from the trash in an online treasure hunt? The following guidelines can help teachers refine the decision-making process (Riedling, 2007).

1. Determine the extent of online information needed to support teaching and learning.

2. Access the needed online information effectively and efficiently with available tools.

3. Evaluate online information and its sources critically.

4. Incorporate selected information into meaningful learning experiences for students.

5. Use information effectively to accomplish specific instructional purposes.

Furthermore, online material must be critically evaluated for authenticity, reliability, relevance, and timeliness. Teachers can use the criteria, shown in figure 4.2, to effectively evaluate online information (Teacher Tap, n.d.).

Summary

Challenging, clear, and appropriate learning materials can increase the likelihood that students will learn the content. This chapter explored some of the significant ideas and questions that teachers must consider when selecting instructional materials, such as how the materials are aligned with curriculum standards; whether they are developmentally appropriate, authentic, and bear real meaning to students' lives; and the criteria used to judge the accuracy and rigor of online resources.

To close, we provide several handouts to help teachers in their journey toward selecting and designing meaningful and purposeful learning materials.

Using the nine principles defined by Jan Herrington, Thomas Reeves, and Ron Oliver (2010), the "Authentic Learning Materials" handout (page 50) can provide teachers with strategies to select and create authentic learning materials for students. Consider the nine principles as nine techniques to make learning meaningful and authentic. Teachers should select the techniques that apply to their specific lesson or unit and determine how to put them into practice.

The handout "Developing Appropriate Learning Materials" (page 52) offers three graphs based on the application of Vygotsky's (1978) zone of proximal development. These graphs can help teachers select and design

Criteria	Questions to Ask
Authority: Know the author and publisher.	• Who created this information, and what is the purpose of the material—to inform, persuade, sell, and so on? • Do you recognize this author or his/her work? Is he/she qualified? • What expertise does he/she have in this area? • Does the author acknowledge other viewpoints and theories?
Objectivity: Think about perspectives.	• Is the information based on fact or opinion? • Is the tone objective or subjective? • Is the information biased in any identifiable respect? • How does the sponsorship impact the perspective of the information? • Does it present a balanced perspective?
Authenticity and Credibility: Know the source.	• Where does the information originate—an established organization or author? • Has the information been reviewed by others for accuracy? • Is this a primary or secondary source of information? • Are original sources well cited and documented?
Timeliness: Consider the currency of the information.	• Does it provide specific dates of publication and updates? • Does currency matter with your particular topic?
Content and Relevance: Consider how the information can enhance teaching.	• Does the information contain the required breadth and depth? • Is the information written in a form that students can understand? • Is the information organized and presented in a meaningful and appealing way? • Is the information useful for accomplishing your instructional objectives?

Source: Adapted from Teacher Tap, n.d.

Figure 4.2: Criteria for evaluating and selecting online instructional resources.

appropriate learning materials to promote student learning as well as determine students' performance levels.

The handout "Selecting and Evaluating Online Sources" (page 53) is based on Ann Marlow Riedling's (2007) framework of information literacy, as well as the work of other researchers (Branch, Kim, & Koenecke, 1999). Teachers can use these guidelines to assess and reflect on the process of selecting and evaluating online sources to meet students' needs. If teachers want to teach students information literacy skills, they can adapt these guidelines to create an assessment rubric.

Authentic Learning Materials

	Yes/No	Notes (How would you implement it?)
1. Provide authentic contexts (either physical or virtual) that reflect the way the knowledge is used in real life. Characteristics: • Preserve the complexity of the real-world setting. • Provide the purpose and motivation for learning. • Allow ideas, concepts, and skills to be formed in the context of real situations. Examples: Present real-world problems, such as lack of justice, climate change, and so on, in a simulation.		
2. Provide authentic tasks and activities that are relevant to students' lives. Characteristics: • Provide clear goals and real-world relevance. • Promote production of knowledge rather than reproduction. • Provide complex and ill-defined problems. Examples: Plan a simulated trip to a country being studied; design a play for a literature unit being studied.		
3. Provide access to expert performance and process modeling. Characteristics: • Provide access to the way an expert would think and act. • Provide assessment to learners in various levels of expertise. • Provide opportunities for the sharing of narratives and stories. Examples: Use online websites for access to expert opinions, lectures, and presentations in podcasts or TED Talks.		
4. Provide multiple roles and perspectives. Characteristics: • Provide multiple perspectives, not just a single perspective such as a textbook. • Use powerful search tools to encourage a range of views. • Provide varied forms of media on the web. Examples: Use online search engines, databases, libraries, and newspaper editorials.		

Instructional Planning for Effective Teaching © 2016 Solution Tree Press • solution-tree.com
Visit **go.solution-tree.com/instruction** to download this page.

	Yes/ No	Notes (How would you implement it?)
5. Provide opportunities for joint problem solving and social support for collaborative construction of knowledge. Characteristics: • Have students work in teams or pairs rather than individually. • Construct learning activities for student groups, not individuals. Examples: Apply online collaborative writing tools such as wikis, Dropbox, blogs, and Blackboard.		
6. Promote reflection to think about and discuss choices. Characteristics: • Provide opportunities to make choices. • Provide opportunities to reflect in journals and diaries. Examples: Write journal and diary entries.		
7. Promote articulation to make tacit knowledge explicit. Characteristics: • Present an argument to defend a position or idea with evidence, either orally or in writing. Examples: Work with an online forum such as Twitter; develop documentaries, blogs, presentations, and posters.		
8. Provide coaching and scaffolding at critical times. Characteristics: • Do not attempt to transmit knowledge. • Rather than lecture, take a supportive and facilitative role. Examples: Show students the outcome or product before they complete it; use think-alouds, graphic organizers, and questioning.		
9. Provide for authentic assessment of learning within tasks. Characteristics: • Integrate assessment and learning activities. • Provide opportunities to craft polished performances. • Extend periods of time for finishing tasks. Examples: Develop projects, portfolios, presentations, and reports.		

Source: Adapted from Herrington, J., Reeves, T. C., & Oliver, R. (2010). A guide to authentic e-learning. New York: Routledge.

Developmentally Appropriate Learning Materials

Add or delete levels from the scale of progression as needed. Provide descriptions of what each level of performance looks like in student learning. Identify each student's current level, goal, and strategies for promotion to the next level.

Knowledge or skill objective: _____

Learning materials or strategies: _____

Novice	Apprentice	Practitioner	Expert
_____	_____	_____	_____
_____	_____	_____	_____
_____	_____	_____	_____

Use the graph to describe what students can already do, what they cannot do even with assistance, and what they can do with guidance or collaboration with more capable peers. Consider the zone of proximal development—the knowledge or skills should be challenging but achievable with assistance.

Knowledge or skill objective: _____

Learning materials or strategies: _____

What students can do

Zone of proximal development

What students can't do

Identify your criteria to evaluate whether the learning materials are too easy, too hard, or just right.

Knowledge or skill objective: _____

Just right: _____

Learning materials or strategies: _____

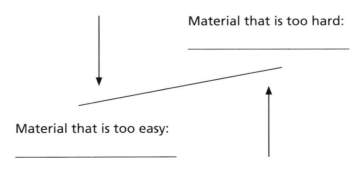

Material that is too hard:

_____

Material that is too easy:

_____

Instructional Planning for Effective Teaching © 2016 J. H. Stronge • solution-tree.com

Visit **go.solution-tree.com/instruction** to download this page.

Selecting and Evaluating Online Sources

	Very Poor	Poor	OK	Good	Very Good
Determined the nature and extent of the information needed					
I defined the need for information during the planning process and knew what I was looking for.					
I identified a variety of types and formats of potential sources of information.					
I considered the availability, feasibility, costs, and benefits of acquiring the needed information.					
I evaluated the nature and extent of the potential information according to my students' learning needs.					
Accessed the information effectively and efficiently					
I selected the most appropriate information retrieval systems for accessing the needed information.					
I effectively implement a variety of search strategies.					
I refined the search strategies as needed.					
I extracted, recorded, and managed the information and its sources.					
Evaluated information and its sources critically and incorporated selected information into a meaningful learning experience					
I developed and applied initial criteria for evaluating both the information and its sources.					
I evaluated the accuracy of the information and made sure it was free from bias and exaggerated statements.					
I assessed whether the new information would have an impact on students' value systems and took steps to reconcile these differences.					
I evaluated whether the level of information was appropriate for my students' reading and developmental levels.					
I made sure to select information that was clearly presented.					
I made sure the information aligned to the content, learning objectives, activities, and procedures.					
I selected information that was complete in scope and ready for use. I reorganized other information to make sure it was incorporated into and coherent with my whole package of instructional materials.					

page 1 of 2

	Very Poor	Poor	OK	Good	Very Good
I validated my own understanding and interpretation of the information through discourse with colleagues or external subject-area experts when needed.					
Used the information effectively to accomplish specific instructional purposes					
I used the information effectively to accomplish at least one specific instructional purpose.					
I used the information in combination with an effective instructional strategy.					
I used information that enhanced student engagement.					
I used the information to develop students' higher-order thinking skills such as critical thinking.					

Sources: Adapted from Branch, R. M., Kim, D., & Koenecke, L. (1999). Evaluating online educational materials for use in instruction *(ERIC Digest No. ED430564). Accessed at http://files.eric.ed.gov/fulltext/ED430564.pdf on April 30, 2015; Riedling, A. M. (2007).* An educator's guide to information literacy: What every high school senior needs to know. *Westport, CT: Libraries Unlimited.*

Instructional Planning for Effective Teaching © 2016 Solution Tree Press • solution-tree.com

Visit **go.solution-tree.com/instruction** to download this page.

Chapter 5

Using Student Learning Data for Planning

Planning is preparation for action. Without prior thinking and planning, ongoing review, adjusting as plans unfold in practice, reflecting on what worked and what didn't, and making changes based on those reflections, teachers seldom improve practice. Thus, effective teachers must consider a variety of factors when planning instruction. One of the key issues to consider is how to use student assessment data to help determine what to teach and to whom. Student learning data contribute to teachers' decisions in planning lessons, grouping students for instruction, and diagnosing the strengths and weaknesses of individual students (Young & Kim, 2010). In addition, student data allow teachers to know what and how well their students have learned.

The feasibility of a particular lesson largely depends on content goals and mandated objectives, time, material resources, and especially, students' prior performance. Many of these factors constrain teachers in ways that are beyond their immediate control. For example, there is a prescribed, fixed amount of time each day in which formal instruction may occur. Typically, hours of the day are chunked into units dedicated to the study of certain subjects or disciplines as determined by a legislative body, school board, or school administrator. This means that if teachers are to maximize student learning, they must operate within these constraints and be as efficient as possible; this is where using student learning data comes to bear.

An optimum planning approach is to create adaptive plans by diagnosing student learning needs in specific areas, developing learning activities that conform to evolving student skill levels, and adjusting the time and pace in a content area according to student performance. Using student learning data for planning involves a purposeful way of scheduling and rescheduling learning experiences by incorporating additional practice and review in order to increase the study time allocated to challenging content areas and increase student learning outcomes.

What Research Says About Student Learning Data

Katherine Misulis (1997) comments that "regardless of the teaching model and methods used, effective instruction begins with careful, thorough, and organized planning on the part of the teacher" (p. 45). Comparing the planning practices of less effective teachers versus effective teachers, numerous research studies find that less effective teachers have more difficulty responding to individual student needs in their planning. They tend to develop a one-size fits-all approach to planning, whereas more experienced, effective teachers build in differentiation and contingencies at different points during the lesson (Good & Brophy, 2007; Jay, 2002; Livingston & Borko, 1989; Sabers et al., 1991; Sawyer, 2011).

As an illustration, Glenda Haynie (2006) examines the planning practices of ten effective and ten less effective teachers whose effectiveness was determined by their success in facilitating student achievement gains from one year to another on standardized tests. She finds that seven of the ten top teachers say they collaborate with one or more teachers while planning for instruction;

however, six of the ten less effective teachers report that they always plan lessons alone. The top teachers also report that they use some or no suggested, prepared resources to plan their own activities, while less effective teachers tend to fully rely on prepared resources. In addition, all the ten top teachers use student data in instructional planning. They use the data they collect themselves and the data from the school and district administration to make informed decisions about what goals and objectives to address. However, the teachers at the bottom report that they have no time for data.

Unfortunately, teacher preparation programs are too frequently ill matched to new teachers' needs for assessment. Teachers also report that in-service professional development that focuses on using student data is infrequent. This means that both preservice preparation and in-service development leave teachers with a substantial student assessment skill deficiency. Thus, teachers' practice of assessing and using assessment data tend to be individual and learned on the job through trial and error, leaving substantial unevenness in teachers' assessment skills and practices (Young & Kim, 2010).

The practice of planning with student learning data is essential for effective instruction. High-quality assessment data give teachers information regarding the extent to which students have attained the intended learning outcomes, and they inform teachers' instructional decision making as well. The goals of using data are to provide teachers with evidence of student learning to facilitate informed decisions about revising instruction and advancing student learning. Various research studies find that when teachers use student data on a regular basis, they effect greater student achievement than teachers who use conventional monitoring methods and experience more improvement in their instructional structure; their pedagogical decisions reflect greater realism and responsiveness to student progress; and students are more knowledgeable of their own learning and more conscious of learning goals and progress (Fuchs, Deno, & Mirkin, 1984; Fuchs & Fuchs, 2003).

Research indicates that teachers who incorporate student data into their instructional decisions can effect substantial achievement gains. Influential reviews of research by Gary Natriello (1987), Terence Crooks (1988), and Paul Black and Dylan Wiliam (1998) demonstrate that substantial student learning gains are possible when teachers introduce assessment results into their classroom practice. In their research review, Black and Wiliam (1998) examine a multitude of empirical

studies in which teachers use explicit procedures for reviewing data and determining next steps based on the analysis. They find that the formative use of assessment results has substantial positive effects on student achievement, with the effect size ranging from 0.3 to 0.7 standard deviations. Particularly, they find that formative assessment is more effective for low achievers than other students, thus helping reduce achievement gaps while raising achievement overall at the same time (Stronge & Xu, 2012).

Additional research finds that the use of assessment data is more likely to have a positive influence on student learning when they possess the following six characteristics (Black & Wiliam, 1998; Stiggins & DuFour, 2009).

1. Align with the framework of learning targets and instruction

2. Have sufficient validity and reliability to produce an accurate representation of student learning

3. Are accompanied by frequent information feedback rather than infrequent judgmental feedback

4. Involve students deeply in classroom review and monitoring

5. Communicate processes and results in a timely and effective manner

6. Are documented through proper recordkeeping of learning results

How to Move From Research to Practice

Any good teacher knows that the practice of assessing and documenting student learning is essential for effective instruction and learning. Using student data determines the effectiveness of a period of teaching (for example, a lesson, unit, semester, or school year) in terms of student learning and provides a basis for continuing instruction. Additionally, collecting evidence of student learning provides teachers with day-to-day data on students' mental preparedness for certain learning targets and facilitates data-based decisions for instructional modification (Stronge & Xu, 2012).

Collecting Student Learning Data

To gain a deeper understanding of student learning, teachers can collect data from multiple sources, such as annual state assessments, interim district and school assessments, and classroom-performance data such as teacher-student questioning, whole-class discussion, journal entries, portfolio entries, exit cards, skill inventories, pretests, homework assignments, student opinion, or interest surveys (Bongiorno, 2011; Tomlinson, 1999). In addition, reviewing student work (for example, student writing samples and project-based work) is an important way of assessing student performance on curricular goals and identifying desired changes in instructional practices. Considering assessment in terms of a time frame, student learning data can be generated and collected through three broad types of assessments: diagnostic, formative, and summative.

Diagnostic assessment ascertains, prior to instruction, each student's strengths, weaknesses, knowledge, and skills, and permits the teacher to remediate, accelerate, or differentiate the instruction to meet each student's readiness for new learning.

Formative assessment is integral to the instructional process to help teachers adjust and modify their teaching practices to reflect the progress and emerging needs of students.

Finally, summative assessment occurs at the end of a major learning unit, semester, or school year to determine student attainment of the standards and outcomes of subject areas or learning goals.

Using Student Learning Data for Planning

A teacher's data skills mean more than merely testing students or measuring achievement. Researchers usually draw a distinction between assessment *of* learning and assessment *for* learning. Norman Gronlund (2006) describes assessment *of* learning as a broad category that includes all of the various methods for determining the extent to which students are achieving the intended learning outcomes of instruction. In contrast, assessment *for* learning involves the teacher gathering, analyzing, and using data to measure learner progress, guide instruction, and provide timely feedback (Stronge & Xu, 2012).

Effective teachers not only collect student learning data (assessment *of* learning), but they also use the data systematically and intelligently (assessment *for* learning).

Data collection is a waste of time and effort if the results are shelved and collect dust. The value is in how data can lead to improvement in teaching and learning (Kerr, Marsh, Ikemoto, Darilek, & Barney, 2006). Thus, teachers can engage in the indispensable practice of using student learning data to continuously evaluate the effectiveness of their teaching and make more informed instructional decisions (Safer & Fleischman, 2005). Student learning data can facilitate instructional planning in many ways, including the following (Fuchs & Fuchs, 2003; Gronlund, 2006).

- Providing diagnostic information regarding students' mental readiness for learning new content

- Providing formative and summative information needed to monitor student progress and adjust instruction

- Keeping students motivated

- Holding students accountable for their own learning

- Identifying students in need of additional or different forms of instruction

- Enhancing instructional decision making by assessing the adequacy of student progress

- Prompting teachers to build stronger instructional programs that are more varied and responsive to students' needs

Figure 5.1 (page 58) shows a chart created by April McDonnagh, a fourth-grade mathematics teacher. Following is McDonnagh's reflection on the chart, which indicates ongoing integration between planning and assessment on a regular basis.

> The idea for this chart comes from our webinar series on differentiation for mathematics. The idea is to preassess students not only with the objectives for the current unit but also include one or two essential skills from a previous year and one or two challenge objectives. I then use various "quick checks" throughout the unit to determine when students have mastered certain objectives and record the date so that I have an accurate record. I also can determine when students need extra challenges. This particular class is very diverse, so I decided to try it first with them.

Unit Dates: November 3–28

R = Remediation necessary   E = Emerging skills   P = Progressing skills   C = Challenge needed

Student	1	2	3	4	5	6	7	8	9	10	11	12	13	14	15	16	17	18	19	20	21	22	23
Preassessment Level	R	R	R	R	R	E	E	E	E	E	E	E	E	E	E	E	E	P	P	P	C	C	C
CCSS Math Content 3.OA.C.7: Fluently multiply and divide within 100.	11/14–chart 12/10–full	11/17–chart 12/15–full	11/10–chart 03/19–full	11/05–chart 01/16–full	11/10–chart	Mastered on preassess																	
By the end of grade 3, know from memory all products of two one-digit numbers.						↑			↑			↑			↑			↑			↑		
CCSS Math Content 4.OA.A.1: Interpret a multiplication equation as a comparison; represent verbal statements of multiplicative comparisons as multiplication equations.	11/21	11/23	11/25	11/23	11/23	11/14	11/14	11/14	11/18	11/14	11/14	11/16	11/14	11/17	11/14	11/14	11/14	Mastered on preassess					
CCSS Math Content 4.OA.A.2: Multiply to solve word problems involving multiplicative comparisons . . .	11/17 *	11/17 *	11/21 *	11/21 *	12/03 *	11/17	11/17	11/17	11/17	11/17	11/19	11/18	11/19	11/20	11/17	11/17	11/17	Mastered on preassess					
CCSS Math Content 4.OA.A.3: Solve multistep word problems posed with whole numbers and having whole-number answers using the four operations . . .	11/28 *	11/28 *	11/27 *	12/06 *	11/24 *	11/24	11/24	11/24	11/26	11/25	11/25	11/24	11/24	11/24	11/24	11/24	11/26	Mastered on preassess					
CCSS Math Content 4.OA.B.4: Find all factor pairs for a whole number in the range 1–100 . . . Determine whether a given whole number in the range 1–100 is prime or composite.	11/24	11/25	11/27	12/10	12/15	11/21	11/21	11/21	11/21	11/21	11/24	11/24	11/25	11/25	11/21	11/21	11/21	11/23	11/23	11/23	Mastered on preassess		
CCSS Math Content 4.NBT.B.5: Multiply a whole number of up to four digits by a one-digit whole number, and multiply two two-digit numbers . . .	11/17–chart 12/15–full	11/17–chart 12/15–full	11/17–chart 12/03–full	12/12–chart 01/03–full	11/24–chart	11/17	11/17	11/17	11/18	11/11	11/17	11/17	11/17	11/18	11/17	11/21	11/24	11/23	11/17	11/17	Mastered on preassess		
Challenge Skill: CCSS Math Content 5.NBT.B.5: Fluently multiply multidigit whole numbers using the standard algorithm.																		11/19	11/20	11/20	11/10	11/06	11/11
Postassessment Score	65	40	80	65	55	40	60	70	80	85	875	70	60	825	90	100	95	925	85	825	100	95	100
Postassessment Retest (if lower than 70% originally)	75	65		70	70	65	70	80					75							90	N/A	N/A	N/A

lunch tutoring

* = Accommodations such as multiplication chart or calculator allowed in order to determine understanding of concepts.

▢ = Modified grading plan or accommodation on assessment as outlined by IEP.

Source: James H. Strong. Used with permission.

Figure 5.1: Sample unit assessment chart—Fourth-grade mathematics.

Students who score lower than 70 percent mastery are required to wait a week (during which we review further) and retake the assessment. Anyone who scores below an A can retake the assessment if they want to, and I provide extra practice for them to do at home, but it is not required.

I realized that some of my students already had the objectives for this unit mastered. I modified some of my plans by differentiating the lessons for those students at remediation and challenge levels with some ideas from the webinar, but I still felt like I could be doing more. It prompted me to work with the third-grade mathematics teacher who uses small groups and centers for her students. This helped me better differentiate based on the preassessments. I started trying out small groups during December and really got into the swing of it by January.

The webinar also pointed out that you can't just stop teaching students who haven't mastered the objectives because it's time to move on, especially in something like mathematics in which the skills build on one another. For instance, if students don't understand multiplication, they're going to struggle with fractions. I continued working with some of my struggling students on certain skills until they were able to grasp them. Without assessing students in this manner, I could not have modified my instruction to better meet their needs. This is another reason I wanted to start using small groups—so I can keep working with students on objectives as long as needed.

Using this method of formative/summative assessment for my students has changed the way I teach mathematics. I'm excited to start next year doing this from the beginning. I saw huge gains in my students' progress once I implemented this system, and I can't wait to see what happens when I start it from day one. (A. McDonnagh, personal communication, April 26, 2014)

Applying Student Data to Learning Goals

Setting goals for student learning is a planning strategy that systematically guides instructional modifications. It is a process that helps teachers use student learning data to continuously evaluate the effectiveness of their teaching and make more informed instructional decisions. Goal setting typically begins with a preassessment to pinpoint students' current performance level on skills or depth-of-content knowledge in relation to the curriculum.

After preassessment data are analyzed, the teacher has the information necessary to devise learning goals that reflect mastery of the curriculum content and skills for groups and individual students. The teacher then uses the preassessment data to create a student learning goal. Once he or she creates the goal, the teacher selects the most effective instructional strategies to help students attain that goal. After implementation, the teacher monitors these instructional strategies for effectiveness. He or she refines or revises strategies, as necessary, based on student performance and progress. At the end of the course or year, the teacher administers a postassessment to ascertain whether the goal has been achieved (Stronge & Grant, 2013). The intent of setting student learning goals is the following (Tucker & Stronge, 2005).

- Make explicit the connection between teaching and learning

- Make instructional decisions based on student data

- Increase the effectiveness of instruction via continuous professional growth

- Focus attention on student results

- Increase student achievement

Summary

Student data speak volumes about what students know, what gaps they have in learning, and what teachers can do to meet their academic needs. When teachers have the awareness and expertise to appropriately analyze and interpret these data, the data can empower instructional planning in a significant and positive way. No single source of data can tell teachers all they need to know about their students' learning, therefore, teachers must use information from multiple sources—such as diagnostic, formative, and summative assessments—to inform their instruction as well was when and what to review, adjust, and reteach.

To close, we provide several handouts to help teachers in their journey toward using student learning data for instructional planning.

There is a vast amount of data and data sources available to teachers. The handout "Using Formative Data for Instructional Planning" can help teachers evaluate how to use student learning data to more effectively inform their instructional planning.

The handout "Assessing Your Assessment Practices" (page 62) provides statements regarding various instructional planning practices related to student learning data. This tool gives teachers the opportunity to indicate the importance of each practice and assess the frequency with which they use these practices in the instructional planning process.

In the process of classroom instruction, a teacher must make decisions regarding how to pace learning activities and allocate instructional time. At some point, the teacher must make a fundamental decision about whether the class as a whole, in small groups, or as individual students can meet the lesson objectives. When should a teacher decide to move on to the next goal? Should he or she wait until every single student in the class masters the new content or skill? The handout "Percentage Mastery Formula for New Learning" (page 63) provides a percentage mastery formula that can assist teachers in using student learning data to decide when to present new learning.

Using Formative Data for Instructional Planning

Select three data sources. Then, explain how you are currently using these data. Finally, describe how you might use these data more formatively for instructional planning.

Data Source	How are you currently using these data?	How might you use these data more formatively for instructional planning?
Example: End-of-Unit Mathematics Assessments	I grade the tests, enter the grades in the grading grid, and return them to students for parent signature.	After grading the tests, I could look at the results again to identify patterns in student performance. I could determine if there are some concepts with which students are not yet showing mastery, and then adjust plans for subsequent lessons to revisit those concepts. I also could identify if there are patterns in the kinds of questions students are having difficulty with (for example, short answer or multiple choice). I could highlight two to three problems that I want each student to look at again to see if he or she can identify the problem. If the student identifies his or her error, I will give half credit.

Assessing Your Assessment Practices

Below is a list of various instructional planning practices related to using student learning data. Indicate how important you believe each practice to be as well as your assessment of the frequency with which you use this practice in planning.

Importance of the practice:

1 = Not Very Important

2 = Somewhat Important

3 = Quite Important

4 = Extremely Important

Frequency of practice:

1 = Rarely

2 = Sometimes

3 = Quite Often

4 = Very Often

Importance of Practice				Practice	Frequency of Practice			
Not very ◀▶ Extremely					Rarely ◀▶ Very Often			
1	2	3	4	Use preassessment/diagnostic data to guide instructional planning	1	2	3	4
1	2	3	4	Use local and state (summative) assessment data to design instruction that meets students' needs	1	2	3	4
1	2	3	4	Use formative assessments to adjust instruction for reteaching, remediation, and enrichment	1	2	3	4
1	2	3	4	Use student learning data to make pedagogical decisions more responsive to student needs	1	2	3	4
1	2	3	4	Maintain sufficient assessment data to support accurate reporting of student progress	1	2	3	4
1	2	3	4	Align data-collection methods to learning goals and standards	1	2	3	4
1	2	3	4	Use student learning data to supervise the overall adequacy of student learning	1	2	3	4
1	2	3	4	Identify specific students in need of additional or different forms of instruction	1	2	3	4

Reflection Questions

1. What gaps did you notice?

    _____

    _____

2. Which skills are important to you but not used frequently in your classroom?

    _____

    _____

Instructional Planning for Effective Teaching © 2016 J. H. Stronge • solution-tree.com

Visit **go.solution-tree.com/instruction** to download this page.

Percentage Mastery Formula for New Learning

Step 1: Percentage Mastery Score

Determine the percentage mastery for your most recent group of students. For example, if 60 percent of students were at or above mastery, then the percentage would be 60.

You could also calculate percentage mastery from the average of a two- or three-unit instruction period. For example, percentage mastery for the last three units of 50 percent, 60 percent, and 55 percent would equal an average score of 55 percent.

Step 2: Discrepancy Mastery Score

Subtract the percentage mastery from the maximum possible score (typically 100 percent). In this example, the calculation for a one-unit score of 60 percent would be:

100 percent – 60 percent = 40 percent

Thus, 40 percent would be the discrepancy between the most recent level of performance (60 percent) and the ideal level of performance (100 percent).

Step 3: Realistic Percentage Mastery Score

Although the ideal performance mastery is for all students to meet or exceed mastery, achieving 100 percent participant mastery, in most instances, is not realistic. Thus, a rule of thumb estimate is to divide the discrepancy score (40 percent) by half.

40 percent ÷ 2 = 20 percent

This yields a more realistic, achievable percentage mastery goal to be employed over three to four units of instruction.

Step 4: Annual Percentage Mastery Score

Divide the realistic percentage mastery score from step 3 by either three or four units, depending on the time frame allocated for achieving improvement in percentage mastery. For example, using a three-unit period, the calculation would be:

20 percent ÷ 3 units = 6.33 percent (or 6 percent) growth in mastery per unit

If the goal is achieved, then the results would be similar to the following example.

- Ideal mastery score: 100 percent

- Beginning mastery score: 60 percent

- Discrepancy mastery score: 40 percent

- Realistic percentage mastery score: 40 percent ÷ 2 = 20 percent

- Per unit percentage mastery score: 20 percent ÷ 3 units = 6 percent per unit (rounded)

    - Unit 1: 60 percent + 6 percent = 66 percent

    - Unit 2: 66 percent + 6 percent = 72 percent

    - Unit 3: 72 percent + 6 percent = 78 percent

Instructional Planning for Effective Teaching © 2016 J. H. Stronge • solution-tree.com
Visit **go.solution-tree.com/instruction** to download this page.

Chapter 6

Designing Engaging Opening and Closing Activities

Planning the opening and closing activities for lessons reminds teachers to think about the priorities of the lesson and how they can best engage all students. Opening and closing activities are opportunities for students to attach personal meaning and relevance to what they learn. These activities can help structure learning and create what psychologists call the primacy-recency effect; that is, during a lesson, learners remember best that which comes first and that which comes last. They remember least that which comes just past the middle (Sousa, 2011). Therefore, the amount of information that students are likely to retain depends on what is presented during the lesson and when. Figure 6.1 shows how the primacy-recency effect influences retention during a forty-minute lesson (Sousa, 2011). The first ten minutes and the last ten minutes of a lesson are the optimal times for learning.

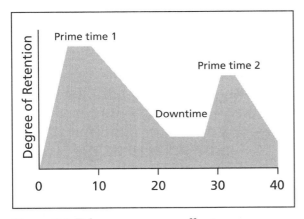

Figure 6.1: Primacy-recency effect.

The primacy-recency effect has important implications for instructional planning and design. It is common for teachers to introduce a lesson objective and then move on to taking attendance, distributing the day's homework, collecting the previous day's homework, and making announcements. By the time new learning finally rolls around, more than ten minutes have lapsed, and students are already beyond optimal learning time. At the end of a lesson, some teachers allow students to do anything they want as long as they keep quiet and stay busy, thus, wasting a learning opportunity. Designing engaging opening and closing activities for instruction provides opportunities for learning as productively and effectively as possible.

What Research Says About Opening and Closing Activities

It is important for both teachers and students to realize that opening and closing activities are essential parts of the overall lesson. These activities weave today's lesson with yesterday's lesson while providing a look ahead at tomorrow's learning. As deliberate parts of the planning process, they summarize new learning, contextualize it, and build anticipation for what comes next. They also serve as important links to establishing and maintaining learning momentum (Lucero, n.d.).

Opening Activities

Several terms used in research describe intriguing and engaging lesson openings, such as *anticipatory set*, *preparatory set*, *hook*, *focusing event*, *advance organizer*, and *expectancy*. When used appropriately, a good opening activity triggers students' interest, curiosity, emotion, and life connections on which the lesson is built. Linda Brupbacher and Dawn Wilson (2008) find that using a brief multimedia presentation, which combines video clips, images, music, or text, can enhance the introduction of a unit or lesson. Opening activities also can serve as motivational tools to arouse student interest in learning new and challenging knowledge and skills. Teacher enthusiasm communicated at the beginning of the lesson can further energize student learning (Akhlaq, Chudhary, Malik, ul-Hassan, & Mehmood, 2010).

Closing Activities

Similarly, how a lesson ends can affect students' ability to organize, evaluate, and store information presented in class. Teachers tend to emphasize hooking students' interest at the start of instruction, while the closure is often hurried and overlooked. On occasion, teachers subconsciously undervalue closure and do not plan for it (Reese, 2014). In many cases, teachers misunderstand the importance of having students participate in the closing portion of instruction. Some teachers summarize the main points in their own words, and consequently, students are deprived of the benefits of engaging in lesson closure (Pollock, 2007).

An earlier study by Rodney Cavanaugh, William Heward, and Fred Donelson (1996) finds that using active review to close a lesson (for example, having students use response cards to answer questions) is significantly more effective than using passive review (for example, having students listen while the teacher projects and reads key lesson points) in facilitating students' recall of learned information.

How to Move From Research to Practice

Opening and closing activities are the most teachable moments in a lesson. It is essential to hold students' attention and provide motivations in the opening and to cue students that they have arrived at an important culminating learning moment in the closure. The following section provides some practical suggestions for helping make lesson openings and closings more compelling.

How to Open a Lesson

The opening of a lesson or learning unit is often intended to introduce the material, stimulate curiosity, and develop a specific direction for the upcoming learning experience. An effective opening piques students' interest and helps them anticipate what they will be learning. Establishing clear learning expectations for students is the key to making lessons fun, intriguing, and entertaining.

The simplest way to succeed with lesson openings is to begin the lesson with an intriguing idea or a key question to engage students. Questions allow teachers to preview and review students' prior knowledge of the subject matter. Another strategy is to establish a purpose or objective for a brief discussion, and then guide students in debriefing ideas related to the lesson plan objective (Vang, 2006). The main purpose of these hooks is to make sure students' minds are ready for the instruction and create an organizing framework for new information. Muhammad Akhlaq et al. (2010) provide some useful guidelines for lesson openings.

- Show a meaningful need for learning the new information, and explain why students need to learn.

- Serve as a connecting link between the present learning and previous learning.

- Reinforce students' desire to learn, showing students how the new knowledge and skills relate to their personal career or life goals.

- Give students specific examples, demonstrating how they will need the information to solve problems or understand future lessons.

- Provide a road map for learning, such as using graphic organizers to show where the lesson is going and how students will get there.

- Clarify what will be covered and what will be left out and why, and how the lesson will be organized; students tend to retain more when they are clear on what to expect.

What comes to mind when you think of a hook? Does it hold or connect to something? Is it sharp? The purpose of a hook is to hold something in place. What do these impressions of hooks have to do with planning for instruction? Opening activities are the hook to hold students in place by piquing their curiosity, engaging their interest, and increasing motivation.

Alan McLean (2003) proposes four guiding factors to help teachers motivate students for learning. These four concepts delve more deeply into what motivates learners and provides a solid foundation for thinking about how we can be deliberate in hooking students to engage them in learning: (1) relevance, (2) manageable challenge, (3) curiosity, and (4) control.

Tasks are engaging to the extent that they are personally meaningful and interesting. Contextualizing learning means being able to see the value and relevance of the skills being learned as opposed to learning that is abstract and divorced from real life. Learning is best placed in meaningful contexts that show its inherent utility to capitalize on students' interests.

Motivating tasks are engaging to the degree that they challenge students' present capacity while permitting some control. The optimal challenge is set just ahead of skill level and takes students beyond their comfort zone. Such a zone of proximal development is the space between what students can do on their own and what they can do with teacher assistance.

Motivating tasks have variety and create curiosity through the element of surprise. Curiosity is elicited with activities that fill the gap in students' present knowledge. Curiosity also depends on providing sufficient complexity so that outcomes are not always certain.

Motivating tasks promote control by allowing a sense of choice and self-determination. Allowing students a choice in activities and participation in establishing rules and procedures fosters a perception of control. Students are not motivated when they believe their actions bear little relationship to outcomes. Exploratory and manipulative activities also give students a sense of control.

How to Close a Lesson

Effective lesson closure serves two major purposes: (1) reinforce what has been learned and (2) assess the level of student learning. This is the time to summarize the main points of the lesson, which can refocus students on what they learned. It also is important to instill a desire and compelling need to retain and use what they learned. Although learning objectives should be reiterated throughout the lesson, the closure is the last chance to emphasize important information (Akhlaq et al., 2010).

Pollock (2007) emphasizes that closure is the time to generalize or summarize the learning. Following are a few guidelines for making closing activities more engaging, student centric, and productive.

- Revisit the learning objectives to reinforce and review key concepts, ideas, or principles.

- Have students discuss important points from the day.

- Prepare an exit card, which asks students to answer key questions, self-rate their understanding, or write one concept they would like to know more about.

- Give students opportunities to draw conclusions from the lesson.

- Discuss in what situations students might be able to use the new information.

- Provide an interesting or unexpected prompt to capture students' interest at the end of the lesson.

- Use the evidence solicited from the closure to decide whether to reteach, add more practice, or move on.

Summary

Openings and closings are significant points in a lesson in which students are encouraged to attach personal meaning and relevance to the content. In this chapter, we examined various practices that teachers can use to promote student interest and motivation, focus students' attention on the lesson and its purpose, and make connections with prior learning and the new learning ahead.

To close, we provide several handouts to help teachers in their journey toward creating engaging opening and closing activities.

Effective opening activities help stimulate student motivation, eagerness, and readiness to learn. They serve as a hook to gain students' attention and interest before content is delivered. Particularly, they trigger students' desire to learn about a specific topic and help create life connections, emotional associations, and common experiences to use as a base for developing ideas and understanding during the lesson or unit that follows (Brupbacher & Wilson, 2008). As with most other instructional techniques, the effectiveness of opening activities depends on how skillfully they are designed and implemented. A teacher's ingenuity and effort in planning are important. The handout "Effective Opening Activities" provides guiding questions to consider and a few tips and suggestions to help facilitate teacher planning (ED491D, n.d.).

Effective closing activities provide an overview (or review) of the learning. They also allow the teacher to assess student learning to inform the planning of future instruction. Closure should take five to ten minutes at most and convey a sense of urgency and focus. The handout "Effective Closing Activities" (page 70) provides examples of closing activities that can be used as a reference for planning (Lucero, n.d.; WriteSteps, n.d.).

Another way to think about opening and closing activities is to use them as preassessments and post-assessments of instruction. The assessment perspective can lead to a number of criteria for making openings and closings more effective. The handout "Opening and Closing Activities as Assessments" (page 71) provides two lists of statements that teachers can use to evaluate the design of instructional openings and closings (Hockett & Doubet, 2014).

Effective Opening Activities

As you design your opening activities, consider the following questions.

1. What can pique students' interest for the subject matter to come?

2. What do students need to know before they can delve into the lesson?

3. How should I inform students of the lesson's context and objective in an understandable way?

Consider these sample activities for use in the opening.

- [ ] Provocative and compelling questions
- [ ] Review of previous lesson
- [ ] Images
- [ ] Story
- [ ] Startling or unexpected statement
- [ ] Visuals, graphic organizers, or thinking maps (for example, KWL)
- [ ] Other: _____

Evaluate the opening against the following checklist.

- [ ] The activity reviews previous learning that is relevant to this lesson.
- [ ] The activity is interesting and motivating.
- [ ] The activity is tied to students' personal experiences.
- [ ] The activity length is reasonable, as long or short as necessary.
- [ ] The activity stresses the value of the lesson.
- [ ] The activity sets the stage for new learning.

Source: Adapted from ED491D. (n.d.). Shooting for success! Madelyn Hunter lesson cycle. *Accessed at http://ed491.weebly.com /uploads/8/4/6/1/8461140/anticipatorysets.pdf on April 30, 2015.*

Effective Closing Activities

3-2-1	Exit Pass
List the following. • Three items students learned • Two items students have a question about • One item students want you to know **Note:** You may use sticky notes, index cards, or other materials.	Have students answer questions in writing or reflect in some way about the learning before leaving the classroom.
Parking Lot	**Postcard**
Give students sticky notes, and ask them to record key words, phrases, or ideas from the lesson. Then have them "park" their sticky notes in the designated "parking lot" for others to preview. Review the parking lot for closure.	Give students an index card. Have them write a postcard to their parents explaining about the day's lesson.
Asking Questions	**I Care Why?**
Ask students the following. • What one thing did you learn today? • How does today's lesson impact your understanding? • How would you summarize today's lesson for someone who wasn't here? • What was the most significant learning from today? • What aha moment did you have today? • What was the most difficult concept in today's lesson?	Have students explain the relevancy of the new information to their lives and how they might use it.

Sources: Adapted from Lucero, R. (n.d.). Closure activities: Making that last impression. Accessed at http://teaching.colostate.edu/tips /tip.cfm?tipid=148 on April 30, 2015; WriteSteps. (n.d.). Closure activities. Accessed at www.writestepswriting.com/Portals/0 /newsletter/pdf/Closure_Activities.pdf on April 30, 2015.

Opening and Closing Activities as Assessments

Openings as Preassessments					Closings as Postassessments				
Very Poor ⟵			⟶ Very Good		Very Poor ⟵			⟶ Very Good	
1	2	3	4	5	1	2	3	4	5
Serve as an invitation to the coming learning experience, not a setback					Serve as opportunities to reinforce what students have just learned				
Pique students' interest in what they are about to learn					Reiterate the goals and objectives of the lesson or unit				
Include just a few key questions (not long or complicated)					Communicate clearly the criteria for reaching the goals and objectives successfully				
Align with key lesson or unit goals—facts, skills, and understandings that are essential for students to know					Elicit information about learning, provide troubleshooting, and use the evidence to inform planning of coming instruction				
Are accessible to all students rather than selected advanced learners					Gain insight into the degree and depth of student understanding				
Tap into students' minds to draw out what they know and misunderstand					Encourage students to reflect and demonstrate metacognitive thinking about their learning				
Uncover the prerequisite knowledge and skills students must possess to meet the requirements of the coming lesson or unit without great struggle					Help students understand it is important to provide evidence of their own learning through their work and keep records of their work to mark progress				

Source: Adapted from Hockett, J. A., & Doubet, K. J. (2014). Turning on the lights: What pre-assessments can do. Educational Leadership, 71(4), 50–54.

Part II

Strategies for Effective Instructional Planning

Part II of this book comprises six chapters on various topics related to instruction. Instead of focusing on the nuts and bolts of planning and designing unit and lesson plans, these chapters cover broader issues that play an important role in planning instructional design. Chapter 7 discusses long-term strategic planning. It is hard to imagine navigating the Appalachian Trail between Springer Mountain in Georgia and Mount Katahdin in Maine without a map or a compass. The same is true about teaching and learning. Strategic planning can help teachers visualize the big goals that students are expected to achieve, and sequence and time steps appropriately to reach those goals.

Part II also includes two chapters on differentiating instructional planning for diverse learners. Chapters 8 and 9 specifically target students on the two ends of the learning spectrum—gifted and high-ability learners and learners who are struggling. Teachers must know who students are and whom they are teaching before they can match instruction with students' individual needs. Chapter 10 explores planning for instruction and learning that approach a theme, issue, question, or topic using methods and analytical perspectives from more than one academic discipline. Chapter 11 focuses on planning for learning experiences that are enhanced by and integrated with technology. Teachers can use technology to facilitate learning at the lowest level of the cognitive taxonomy when they simply use it to store or display materials. However, teachers can also use technology to foster higher-ordering learning by engaging students in actively synthesizing and using materials for relatively complex projects. The final chapter covers team planning, which focuses on how teachers can work together on collaborative inquiry, instructional planning and practices, and improved student learning.

Chapter 7
Strategic Planning for Teachers

In his bestselling book *The 7 Habits of Highly Effective People*, Covey (1989) emphasizes starting "with the end in mind" (p. 95). In fact, he claims that effective leaders always play out an event twice—once in their heads and then again in reality. This concept of focusing on the big picture—starting with the end in mind—applies equally well to effective teachers. In fact, evidence suggests that effective teachers start the academic year by considering where their students are and where they need to be by the end of the term or year. Effective teachers are strategic planners.

Teaching is a complex activity that involves careful preparation and planning, for both short-term and long-term learning purposes. Misulis (1997) states that "regardless of the teaching model and methods used, effective instruction begins with careful, thorough, and organized planning on the part of the teacher" (p. 45). Like all other design professionals, such as architects, teachers must perform within the constraints of standards and with limited time and other resources.

Strategic planning for teachers focuses on big picture planning, that is, long-term planning for instruction and learning (for example, planning for the whole course or the school year). It helps teachers be proactive in identifying teaching and learning priorities and guides the design of instruction and assessment.

What Research Says About Strategic Planning

Strategic planning is an essential process for teachers to map out the content, skills, assessments, resources, and alignment to one another and to curriculum standards. The process prompts teachers to examine student learning horizontally, vertically, and cyclically. It also helps them make important overarching decisions about teaching and learning.

Curriculum Mapping

Curriculum mapping is a calendar-based planning process in which teachers record the content and skills to teach, how long they plan to teach them, and how the learning matches the intended standards (Jacobs, 1997). Curriculum mapping is a sort of blueprint showing how to address the curriculum during available instruction time (McEwan, 2002). Research solidly documents teachers' positive perceptions of curriculum mapping as an effective strategic planning and curriculum alignment tool.

Ralph Lucas (2005) finds that teachers perceive curriculum mapping as an effective tool for long-range planning. Curriculum mapping can help teachers accomplish the following.

- Plan for students with different ability levels, backgrounds, and developmental needs
- Plan appropriate long-range learning and developmental goals for students
- Sequence appropriate instructional units of study
- Develop appropriate time lines for the completion of instructional units
- Organize instructional materials and resources
- Evaluate students' progress and achievement
- Maintain necessary records of long-range planning efforts

Studies also find a positive relationship between curriculum mapping and improved student achievement (Fairris, 2008; Shanks, 2002). Strategic planning emphasizes developing coherent and progressive units in advance to make intradisciplinary connections (McEwan, 2002). The process of connecting curriculum to instructional plans allows teachers to sequence material in order to promote students' cognitive and developmental growth (Panasuk, Stone, & Todd, 2002).

Curriculum-Learning Connection

Research on long-term planning also highlights the need to plan instruction based on both the curriculum and student learning needs. A quality instructional program should be faithful to the established curriculum (what should be taught) as well as to the learning needs of students (what needs to be learned). In making this curriculum-learning connection, it is important to use knowledge of available resources to determine student needs to acquire or develop established knowledge or skills (Buttram & Waters, 1997).

Timothy Graeff (2010) states that the primary aim of strategic planning is to first identify the overall goals and then identify the strategies, individual activities, and resources necessary to achieve those goals. He also mentions that in order to make learning relevant and meaningful for students, the planning process should not just focus on subject content. Strategic planning begins by identifying students' long-term academic and life goals and then determining the skills and behaviors needed to achieve those goals.

The connection between learning and students' personal goals leads to increased student involvement, attention, and learning (Graeff, 2010). Questions such as the following can be useful to begin strategic planning.

- What might students do with the knowledge ten years from now?

- What skills can students learn from this subject that might help them be college and career ready?

- What are the essential themes and skills in the discipline that make it meaningful and useful?

Mette Huberman et al. (2014) echo this idea, stating that educating for 21st century skills should focus on long-term cumulative knowledge and skills in addition to conventional short-term learning. For example, in a secondary American history course, Jason Endacott (2011) suggests using enduring themes, such as democracy, justice, equality, and freedom, to help students define and understand the parameters of the subject, and then use the themes as a lens to view and compare historical events.

Another example is sixth-grade history teacher Alita Bello, who developed the following mission statement as a method for developing long-term planning in collaboration with students.

> Mission Statement
>
> Sixth-grade ancient history students want to learn new things that we can apply to our future education. We plan to have fun, cooperate, and learn from our mistakes. To do this we will listen, understand, and study to show our best effort in our schoolwork.
>
> We will exceed our own expectations. (A. Bello, personal communication, May 11, 2015)

Bello reflects on the purpose of this mission statement.

> This is the mission statement for our class that we developed at the beginning of the year. Students worked in small groups to explain why they thought they were in school and what they hoped to accomplish this year. Each group then worked with another group to synthesize their thoughts into one statement. And then we worked as a whole class to synthesize again into a final statement that we all agreed on. This posted mission statement allows class members to review values and ensures a common language. We refer to it throughout the year both as a way to determine activities for each unit and to remind ourselves that our actions support our learning. (A. Bello, personal communication, May 11, 2015)

How to Move From Research to Practice

No doubt, there are many ways to plan strategically. No matter which method you use, however, you must think about where you are, where you want to go, and how to get there. Following are two such strategic planning methods: curriculum mapping model and backward design model.

Curriculum Mapping Model

Curriculum development is central to all the processes and experiences occurring in the classroom. However, traditionally, teachers have been excluded from active participation in curriculum development, which has been viewed as within the purview of outside experts. Consequently, there is often a significant difference between the official written curriculum developed by external experts and the actual curriculum implemented in the classroom, because teachers autonomously make choices based on their knowledge, experiences, and the realities in their classroom (Shilling, 2013).

To ensure congruence between the intended and enacted curriculum, Fenwick English (1980) first introduced the concept of curriculum mapping, which delineates "what is actually being taught, how long it is being taught, and the match between what is being taught and the district's testing program" (p. 559).

A large gap can exist between what is specified in the district curriculum guidelines and what is actually taught in the classroom. Curriculum mapping is a technique for gathering data on what is actually being taught through the course of a school year and then matching what's being taught with the targeted curriculum to find the gaps. When operationalized, all teachers at a school enter information about their classroom curricula for the year into a computer database. They enter major activities related to three types of data: content, specific skills, and assessments. By carefully analyzing the maps, teachers can identify and fix curriculum gaps, address repetition, and refine scope-and-sequence connections. They also can identify potential areas for curriculum integration, better align their assessment with state and district standards, and even consider ways to improve teaching strategies and materials. Curriculum mapping as a long-range planning approach can be characterized with the following leveled steps.

Level 1: Curricular Standards and Planning

- Identify a philosophy that guides curriculum implementation.

- Determine the progression of essential content taught.

- Outline modifications of curriculum to special populations.

Level 2: District Curriculum Planning

- Establish content goals keyed to state, district, or school guidelines.

- Determine appropriate teaching activities and assignment strategies.

- Develop appropriate curriculum guides, create an outline for unit plans, and list and sequence major topics.

Level 3: Classroom Units and Lesson Plans

- Establish how curriculum goals are implemented in the classroom.

- Address topics to be covered, materials needed, and activities to be used.

- Identify and develop evaluation strategies.

- Develop and identify adaptations to special populations.

Backward Design Model

Grant Wiggins and Jay McTighe (1998, 2005) offer an alternative approach to instructional planning—the backward design model. Backward design focuses on the idea that instructional planning should begin with identifying the desired results and then working backward to develop instruction. This differs from the traditional approach, which defines what topics must be covered. The Wiggins and McTighe framework identifies three main stages for planning instruction, as shown in figure 7.1 (page 78).

Summary

In this chapter, we discussed how strategic planning allows teachers to examine teaching and learning panoramically through a wide-angle lens. Through strategic planning, teachers can develop a better understanding about the curriculum and student academic needs both horizontally throughout the course of any academic year or vertically over several longitudinal academic years. In this chapter, we also focused on two strategies for long-term planning: curriculum mapping model and the backward design model.

To close, we provide several handouts to help teachers in their journey toward effective strategic planning.

Curriculum mapping reveals the content of teaching, the time to be spent teaching that content, the amount of repetition desired, and the sequence of instruction (English, 1980). *Curriculum alignment*, on the other hand, refers to the congruence between the intended,

---

Stage 1: Identify desired outcomes and results.

Start with the end—the desired results (goals, standards, or benchmarks) and the evidence of learning (performance) called for by the standard or benchmark.

Stage 2: Determine what constitutes acceptable evidence of competency in the outcomes and results (assessment).

Define what forms of assessment demonstrate that students have acquired the desired knowledge, understanding, and skills. Wiggins and McTighe define three types of assessment: (1) performance tasks (authentic tasks of understanding); (2) criteria-referenced assessments (quizzes, tests); and (3) unprompted assessment and self-assessment (observations, dialogues).

Stage 3: Plan instructional strategies and learning experiences that bring students to the desired competency levels.

Determine what sequence of teaching and learning experiences help students develop and demonstrate the desired understanding. Decide on teaching strategies, activities students will participate in during the units, and what resources and materials are needed.

Source: Adapted from Wiggins & McTighe, 1998, 2005.

Figure 7.1: Backward design model.

taught, and experienced curriculum. The handout "Curriculum Alignment" (adapted from Veltri, Webb, Harold, Matveev, & Zapatero, 2011) encourages systematic and iterative design in order to help teachers align expected learning outcomes, learning activities, and assessment criteria.

The handout "Curriculum Mapping" (page 80) can help teachers facilitate the process of generating a holistic and comprehensive view of the curriculum. Template 1 is most appropriate for team planning for vertical alignment of instruction across grades. Template 2 is designed for elementary teachers. Template 3 is designed for secondary teachers for more detailed planning of instructional time.

The handout "Strategic Planning: Self-Assessment" (page 82) is a helpful instrument for teachers in assessing and reflecting on their experiences in strategic planning. The handout also provides a vehicle for evaluating the need for professional development if any areas of weakness are identified through self-assessment.

Curriculum Alignment

Instructions:

1. In the template, write major learning outcomes and unit titles.

2. In the "Intended" and "Assessed" columns, write 1 if they apply to the unit.

3. Add these numbers to get the breadth scores.

4. In the "Enacted" column, write 1 for introduced, 2 for emphasized, 3 for reinforced, or 4 for advanced.

5. Add these numbers to get the depth scores.

6. Compare the breadth and depth scores across units to see if any are off the mark. Examine the last row ("Totals") to ensure all outcomes are adequately covered by planning, instruction, and assessment.

Learning Outcomes

At the end of the academic year or semester, students will be able to:

	Outcome 1:			Outcome 2:			Outcome 3:			Outcome 4:			Breadth Score	Depth Score
	Intended	Enacted	Assessed	Intended	Enacted	Assessed	Intended	Enacted	Assessed	Intended	Enacted	Assessed		
Unit 1														
Unit 2														
Unit 3														
Unit 4														
Unit 5														
Unit 6														
Unit 7														
Unit 8														
Totals														

Source: Adapted from Veltri, N. F., Webb, H. W., Harold, W., Matveev, A. G., & Zapatero, E. G. (2011). Curriculum mapping as a tool for continuous improvement of IS curriculum. Journal of Information Systems Education, 22(1), 31–42.

Curriculum Mapping

Template 1: Collaborative Curriculum Mapping

Grades	Quarter 1	Quarter 2	Quarter 3	Quarter 4

Template 2: Elementary Level

Subject Area	August	September	October	November	December	January	February	March	April	May
Reading										
Writing										
Science										
Mathematics										
Social Studies										

Template 3: Secondary Level

	1	2	3	4	5	6	7	8	9	10	11	12	13	14	15	16	17	18	19	20	21	22	23	24	25	26	27	28	29	30	31
August																															
September																															
October																															
November																															
December																															
January																															
February																															
March																															
April																															
May																															

Block the calendar with the following sample categories and color scheme (you may expand the table by adding information about unit content, and add any categories or colors that work for you):

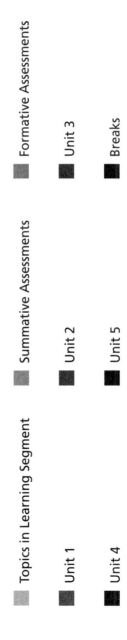

Topics in Learning Segment   Summative Assessments   Formative Assessments

Unit 1   Unit 2   Unit 3

Unit 4   Unit 5   Breaks

Instructional Planning for Effective Teaching © 2016 J. H. Stronge • solution-tree.com
Visit **go.solution-tree.com/instruction** to download this page.

Strategic Planning: Self-Assessment

	Strongly Agree	Agree	Disagree	Strongly Disagree
Strategic planning is a worthwhile process.				
Strategic planning helps me to identify learning goals and objectives.				
Strategic planning helps me to think about the large ideas, issues, and problems of my discipline.				
In addition to focusing on course content, strategic planning helps me to plan from the perspectives of students' career goals, academic goals, and life goals, and identify the skills, behaviors, and abilities needed to achieve those goals.				
Strategic planning helps me to better plot teaching subject knowledge and cognitive skills at the appropriate level.				
Strategic planning helps me to eliminate gaps, redundancies, and unneeded repetitions within grades and subject areas.				
Strategic planning is valuable in ensuring the alignment of intended curriculum and implemented curriculum.				
Strategic planning helps me to improve the congruence between subject content, expected learning outcomes, instructional practices, and assessment methods.				
Strategic planning helps me reflect on instructional design and positively impacts my teaching.				
Strategic planning helps me to sequence learning in a logical and progressive way.				
Strategic planning helps me to articulate the scope and breadth of learning.				
Strategic planning encourages me to seek support and collaboration with other teachers to develop horizontally and vertically coherent instruction.				
Strategic planning helps me to create a product that can be reused as an audit tool to evaluate the effectiveness of my actual instruction execution.				
Strategic planning allows me to work down from big and complex outcomes to specific goals, objectives, and tasks that repond to student needs.				
Strategic planning helps me to maintain balance between accountability of what I am supposed to teach and my autonomy as a professional.				

Instructional Planning for Effective Teaching © 2016 J. H. Stronge • solution-tree.com

Visit **go.solution-tree.com/instruction** to download this page.

Chapter 8

Planning Differentiated Instruction for Gifted and High-Ability Learners

In order for their learning needs to be addressed and their unique talents to flourish, gifted and high-ability students must have differentiated learning experiences appropriate to their individual characteristics, needs, abilities, and interests. Gifted and high-ability learners need consistent opportunities to learn at their challenge level, just as all students do. And just like students with special needs in inclusion classrooms, these highly capable students also have exceptional learning needs and should receive modified versions of learning opportunities. Developing curriculum and instructional strategies that are sufficiently rigorous, challenging, and coherent can be a challenging task, but it is doable—and necessary (Moore, 2005).

Planning differentiated instruction for gifted and high-ability learners must take into account these students' unique needs and abilities, content that must be mastered, and effective instructional strategies. Effective teachers of high-ability learners use a variety of methods, such as acceleration, enrichment, content modification, or curriculum compacting, in order to provide enriching, differentiated activities that foster students' academic growth (Stronge, 2007). But how are teachers to know what to use and when? While planning for differentiation may require greater effort and insight, it is, nonetheless, essential. If we are to match learning opportunities with learning needs for these students, then it is incumbent that we plan appropriately; otherwise, we will continue to miss the mark.

What Research Says About Differentiated Instruction for Gifted and High-Ability Learners

Placing value on appropriately challenging schooling reflects learning theory and research in general, and not just for gifted and high-ability learners. Nevertheless, students, parents, teachers, and various research report that school experiences for gifted learners frequently do not provide sufficient challenges to promote learning (Little, 2012). Research also highlights the curvilinear relationship between boredom and ability, with students at the highest and lowest level of ability most at risk for experiencing boredom (Little, 2012).

In multiple studies, effective teachers of gifted and high-ability learners are found to be highly competent in selecting appropriate high-level materials that could match task complexities and individual skills (Csikszentmihalyi, Rathunde, & Whalen, 1993; Nelson & Prindle, 1992; Shore & Delcourt, 1996). Planning a range of instructional strategies focusing on in-depth learning is a key to properly matching instructional plans with the needs of gifted and highly-ability students (Hansen & Feldhusen, 1994; VanTassel-Baska & Little, 2003).

Effective teachers in general education classrooms facilitate their gifted students' ability to gain access to various resources, such as content-area experts and mentors, pulled-out advanced classes, and counseling (Shore & Delcourt, 1996; Westberg & Archambault, 1997). An international cross-case study indicates that effective teachers of gifted learners place a strong emphasis on planning, with clear connections to assessment. Formal and informal assessment results of student learning influence their planning. These teachers are purposeful in their planning and link objectives and assessment. Additionally, they pay particular attention to variation and flexibility in designing and organizing instructional activities (Stronge, Little, & Grant, 2009).

Another case study finds that exemplary teachers of gifted learners place instructional planning very high on their list of practices for success. They focus on the design phase of teaching, knowing that no single plan or process works for every student. Additionally, they continuously change their actual practices in the classroom—units, lessons, and basic daily work—to reinvent their instruction and maximize learning opportunities (Graffam, 2006).

For nearly fifty years, the field of gifted education has sought to distinguish how effective instruction for high-ability learners is different from effective instruction for general learners. Synthesizing extant research, Jessica Hockett (2009) summarizes five principles that can depict what *advanced* and *challenging* learning looks like—two generic terms often used in describing differentiation for high-ability learners.

- **Principle 1: Use a conceptual approach to organize or explore content that is discipline-based and integrative.**

  - Use the principles, skills, theories, ideas, and values most essential to a field of study to illuminate the nature of the discipline itself.

  - Use the structure of the discipline itself to inform how to arrange learning experiences.

  - Ensure students see where the new learning fits into the larger body of knowledge and from where it originates.

  - Expose students to multiple perspectives, and apply knowledge at multiple levels.

- **Principle 2: Pursue advanced levels of understanding through abstraction, depth, breadth, and complexity.**

  - *Abstraction* involves the ability to work with the implications and extensions of ideas rather than concrete examples and illustrations.

  - *Depth* is defined as intensifying learning, which includes a range of practices, such as using discipline-specific language or examining details, trends, patterns, unanswered questions, rules, ethics, and big ideas. It may involve students pursuing an area of special interest at a high level, studying important issues and problems, or simply spending more time on learning a topic.

  - *Breadth* refers to exposing students to a wide variety of learning experiences within or across a content area or, more simply, extending the core curriculum.

  - *Complexity* refers to making the content more intricately detailed, integrating knowledge and concepts from multiple disciplines, requiring higher-order thinking processes, incorporating multiple perspectives, or having students generate products that need more steps or require advanced resources and skills.

- **Principle 3: Use processes and materials that approximate those of an expert or practicing professional.**

  - Have students engage in authentic research or inquiry-based processes, such as thinking analytically, making decisions, asking questions, generating new ideas, defending ideas, and reconciling opposing viewpoints.

  - Have students assess sophisticated materials for credibility and use higher-level reading or processing skills.

- **Principle 4: Emphasize problems, products, and performances that are true to life and outcomes that are transformational.**

  - Have students propose problems that are significant to individuals, communities, societies, or fields of study.

- Ask students to develop authentic products directed at real audiences and evaluated according to acceptable criteria.

- **Principle 5: Accommodate self-directed learning fueled by student interests, adjustments for pacing, and variety.**

  - Encourage students to investigate areas of interest more in-depth and make choices about the directions and goals of their learning.

  - Increase the pacing of learning by moving students more rapidly through basic skills to accommodate in-depth learning.

  - Use a variety of instructional approaches and materials, content and form, and learning activities.

How to Move From Research to Practice

Gifted learners have a precocious ability to think abstractly and process complex information rapidly. They also have the need to be constantly mentally engaged and to explore subjects in depth. Gifted students' unique academic needs require teachers to incorporate differentiation into instructional planning so that the learning is coordinated with students' development and abilities, regardless of their ages.

Research-Based Classroom Adaptations

Researchers have proposed a variety of ways that the general education classroom environment can be altered to adapt to gifted and high-ability learners. Among the more prominently recommended issues to consider in planning are the following.

Acceleration involves moving through the traditional curriculum at rates faster than usual. Acceleration assumes that different students of the same age are at different levels of learning within and across subject areas. This necessitates determining the learning level and designing learning at a level slightly above it (Brody & Benbow, 1987; Lee, Olszewski-Kubilius, & Pertenel, 2010; Rimm & Lovance, 1992; Steenbergen-Hu & Moon, 2011).

Curriculum compacting is a strategy to streamline the regular learning scope or sequence for high-ability students who can master learning at a faster pace. Teachers can compact content into a shorter time period to eliminate time spent covering materials already mastered by students and replacing them with more rigorous options (Pierce et al., 2011; Reis, Westberg, Kulikowich, & Purcell, 1998).

Enrichment approaches provide deeper and richer learning than the typical student can necessarily master in the available time (Reis et al., 2011; Moon, Feldhusen, & Dillon, 1994; Olenchak, 1995).

Enrichment centers or *learning centers* can serve as focal points for enrichment and acceleration activities (Ibata-Arens, 2012; Lopez & MacKenzie, 1993).

Higher-order learning includes creative- and divergent-thinking activities (Chan et al., 2010) and problem-based learning (Gallagher, Stepien, & Rosenthal, 1992).

Independent study includes guided plans for what and how students can pursue more individualized learning opportunities (Doherty & Evans, 1981; French, Walker, & Shore, 2011).

Advanced Curriculum Units

One powerful model for designing differentiated instruction for gifted learners was developed by a former colleague at the College of William and Mary, Joyce VanTassel-Baska. This integrated curriculum model is solidly researched and involves the teacher designing and implementing *advanced curriculum units*—units specifically developed for gifted and high-ability learners that contain advanced content, high-level process skill development and product generation, and concept-based learning (VanTassel-Baska, 1994; VanTassel-Baska et al., 2002; VanTassel-Baska & Brown, 2007).

Consider VanTassel-Baska's (2002) step-by-step guide on how to plan a differentiated curriculum unit for gifted and high-ability learners.

1. Start with an idea and a related topic (concept, principle, or issue).

2. Outline the idea or create a concept map that defines it more precisely.

3. Refine the outline by reading about the concept and topic.

4. Align the outline with curriculum standards in relevant content areas and revise as appropriate.

5. Determine the level of learners for whom the curriculum is designed (for example, ability, aptitude, functional achievement, and interests).

6. Design learning outcomes and assessments that are tailored to gifted and high-ability learner characteristics.

7. Check for logical consistency, differentiation features, and scope and sequence issues.

8. Design task demands that address each learning outcome.

9. Delineate instructional strategies or models to be employed.

10. Select materials and resources that support the expected learning outcomes.

11. Try out the curriculum unit with a group of gifted or high-ability learners.

12. Revise instruction based on feedback from student performance.

13. Pilot the revised curriculum unit in the classroom.

14. Revise instruction based on pilot results.

15. Field-test the curriculum unit in other classrooms at your school.

While all instructional units for gifted and high-ability learners may not require this extensive planning process, these steps can help guide effective instructional planning. One way to differentiate learning without removing gifted students from their regular heterogeneous classroom is in-class clustering. This option is preferable when only a few students need special accommodations, for example, in schools of relatively small size.

Summary

Teachers in regular education classrooms have the responsibility to recognize giftedness of students and respond to their educational needs. Gifted and high-ability learners tend to be curious about a range of topics, ask thoughtful questions, solve problems in innovative ways, elaborate on ideas, have a sustained span of attention, and persist on complex and challenging tasks. Effective teachers further nurture these characteristics by creating a learning environment where gifted and high-ability learners can engage in activities at their ability levels.

To close, we provide several handouts to help teachers in their journey toward planning differentiated instruction for gifted and high-ability learners.

Gifted learners must have access to instruction that meets their unique learning characteristics. The extensive research in this field has generated a variety of ideas for modifying instruction in ways that are successful with gifted and high-ability learners. Rosalind Walsh, Coral Kemp, Kerry Hodge, and Jennifer Bowes (2012) express the urgent need for teachers to have access to and knowledge of research-based practices in gifted education. The handout "Interventions for Gifted and High-Ability Learners" invites teachers to rate various intervention practices for high-ability learners in regards to their desirability and knowledge needed for implementation.

The handout "Designing Advanced Learning" (page 88) includes a number of options for designing advanced learning for gifted and high-ability learners based on five major recommendations by VanTassel-Baska (2002)—acceleration, complexity, depth, challenge, and creativity. Teachers can review these recommendations as they plan for differentiation and determine if they apply to the specific content area and the needs of high-ability learners in their classrooms.

The handout "Differentiated Instruction Design Template" (page 89) includes components that are featured in literature on differentiated instruction (Johnsen & Ryser, 1996; Sousa & Tomlinson, 2011; Tomlinson & Imbeau, 2010). Teachers can use this template to structure tiered learning experiences for students at different levels of learning readiness.

Interventions for Gifted and High-Ability Learners

Rate the following practices by:

- Level of desirability for implementation
- Level of knowledge needed for implementation (Robinson, Shore, & Enersen, 2007)

Practice	Desirability — This practice will be beneficial to my students, and I want to implement it in my classroom.					Knowledge — I am confident with my knowledge and skills to implement this practice.				
	Disagree ← → Agree					Disagree ← → Agree				
	1	2	3	4	5	1	2	3	4	5
Acceleration										
Advanced-level content and projects										
Authentic, performance-based assessment										
Concept-based teaching or learning experiences organized around major issues, themes, and ideas that define a discipline										
Creative-thinking skills										
Critical-thinking skills										
Cross-disciplinary learning										
Curriculum compacting/compression of content/diagnostic–prescriptive instruction										
Curriculum modifications (depth and breadth)										
Curriculum extension										
Enrichment/learning centers										
Flexible grouping strategies										
Higher-order questioning										
Independent, self-monitored learning										
Inquiry learning										
Integrated language arts										
Metacognitive skills										
Problem finding and identifying										
Problem solving										
Socratic discussion										
Students as practitioners in a field										
Using primary sources										

Reflection

Identify any gaps between the level of desirability to implement a practice and your level of knowledge or confidence in implementing it. What are some professional development actions for improvement?

Source: Adapted from Robinson, A., Shore, B. M., & Enersen, D. L. (2007). Best practices in gifted education: An evidence-based guide. Waco, TX: Prufrock Press.

Instructional Planning for Effective Teaching © 2016 Solution Tree Press • solution-tree.com

Visit **go.solution-tree.com/instruction** to download this page.

Designing Advanced Learning

	Appropriate	Not Appropriate	Notes
Acceleration			
Adjust the pacing of instruction so that high-ability learners don't waste time on learning materials that they already have mastered.	☐	☐	
Use student assessment data to make informed decisions regarding pacing and grouping.	☐	☐	
Complexity			
Include learning activities that involve multiple higher-level thinking skills, such as critical thinking and problem solving.	☐	☐	
Add more variables to make the learning more complex.	☐	☐	
Depth			
Design student learning of an overarching concept in multiple applications (for example, change, systems, patterns, and cause and effect).	☐	☐	
Have students search and analyze multiple resources, including primary resources.	☐	☐	
Have students employ authentic materials and methods to create products.	☐	☐	
Challenge			
Adjust the pacing of instruction so high-ability learners don't waste time on learning materials that they already have mastered.	☐	☐	
Use student assessment data to make informed decisions regarding pacing and grouping.	☐	☐	
Have students make cross-disciplinary applications.	☐	☐	
Be sure learning activities integrate metacognitive skills in the subject areas and provide opportunities for students to reflect and self-evaluate through thinking, discussing, and writing.	☐	☐	
Creativity			
Have students design and construct a product based on principles or criteria.	☐	☐	
Provide opportunities for alternative tasks, products, and assessments.	☐	☐	
Be sure learning outcomes emphasize oral and written communication to a real-world audience.	☐	☐	

Source: Adapted from VanTassel-Baska, J. (2002). Curriculum planning and instructional design for gifted learners. *Denver, CO: Love.*

Instructional Planning for Effective Teaching © 2016 Solution Tree Press • solution-tree.com

Visit **go.solution-tree.com/instruction** to download this page.

Differentiated Instruction Design Template

	Gifted and High-Ability Learners	Traditional Learners	Struggling Learners
Preference: The match between students and learning style or interest			
Content: The knowledge, understanding, and skills students will learn			
Process: Activities through which students make sense of content, including varying the pace of instruction and instructional strategies			
Product: How students demonstrate what they know, understand, and can do after learning			
Environment: Classroom organization, grouping, and the use of other settings			

Sources: Adapted from Johnsen, S. K., & Ryser, G. R. (1996). An overview of effective practices with gifted students in general-education settings. Journal for the Education of the Gifted, 19(4), 379–404; Sousa, D. A., & Tomlinson, C. A. (2011). Differentiation and the brain: How neuroscience supports the learner-friendly classroom. *Bloomington, IN: Solution Tree Press; Tomlinson, C. A., & Imbeau, M. B. (2010).* Leading and managing: A differentiated classroom. *Alexandria, VA: Association for Supervision and Curriculum Development.*

Chapter 9

Planning Differentiated Instruction for Struggling Learners

No two students learn in exactly the same way or at the same pace. And, since students learn at different rates and in different ways for different reasons, effective teachers plan for both academic enrichment and remediation opportunities for their students. For students who may lack the prerequisite knowledge or skills to fully benefit from classroom instruction, the teacher must provide time for them to learn the foundational material on which to build new learning and, then, extend that learning to maximize opportunities for gaining new skills (Stronge, 2007).

Unfortunately, attempts to provide remedial and supplemental instruction to students at risk of school failure have not been very successful, usually because remedial instruction pays too much attention to the deficits of low-achieving students and too little attention to making instruction meaningful (Good & Brophy, 2007). This problem can best be rectified by, first, acknowledging the learning needs of struggling students and, then, focusing on positive solutions to help them succeed. Planning differentiated instruction for struggling learners is based on understanding the characteristics of low-achieving students and providing recommendations for engineering instruction that can reduce students' frustrations and stimulate their interest and success.

What Research Says About Differentiated Instruction for Struggling Learners

Struggling learners are students who are in danger of failing to meet their potential and are identified as less able, disinterested, or refusing to learn. The challenges that struggling students encounter may be caused by many risk factors, including environmental, educational, familial, or internal. Consequently, these students too often develop weak self-efficacy and motivation for academic learning. Frustration and negative feedback have taught them to believe that they don't have the capacity to succeed, even with enormous effort.

Research has found that teachers often assign struggling learners to academic tasks that do not require the demonstration of sophisticated cognitive, social, or self-regulation skills. However, instructional intervention that challenges students to demonstrate academically appropriate skills and communicates high expectancies—such as reading and writing complex texts, sharing opinions with and offering feedback to peers, and monitoring learning progress over extended time periods—can significantly improve student motivation and learning (Miller, 2003).

Motivation and engagement are critical factors in learning, especially for struggling students. Fortunately, evidence suggests that declining motivation can be reversed with instructional practices designed to foster students' self-efficacy (Michaels, Wilson, & Margolis,

2005). Specifically, effective instruction for struggling learners embraces the following three characteristics (Jong, Lin, Wu, & Chan, 2004).

1. Explicit instruction on basic concepts and skills
2. Extensive opportunities to expand the understanding and application of higher-level learning
3. Ongoing progress monitoring for teachers to document student learning and tailor their instruction accordingly

One example of effective instruction for struggling learners is guided practice, which is a technique for improving reading comprehension. Guided practice is characterized by immediate assessment of student performance to determine which segments of the curriculum require additional remediation (Golden, Gersten, & Woodward, 1990). Research also indicates that tiered intervention is an effective approach to helping struggling learners by providing more targeted and appropriate support. Effective tiered intervention strategies depend on accurate diagnostic information and data about what is or is not working for students and what new adjustments can be made, such as moving a student into or out of a more intensive level of support (Duffy, 2007; Heacox, 2012; Roberts, Vaughn, Fletcher, Stuebing, & Barth, 2013).

How to Move From Research to Practice

Differentiated instruction is a teaching theory based on the premise that instructional approaches should vary and be adapted in relation to individual and diverse student needs in the classroom. This means that teachers make vigorous attempts to meet students where they are in the learning process and then move them along as quickly and as far as possible in the context of a mixed-ability classroom (Moore, 2005).

Planning Models for Differentiated Instruction

Approaches to differentiated instruction are far too voluminous to summarize here. However, most evidence-based and field-tested differentiated planning models, particularly modified instruction for struggling learners, incorporate at least the following four elements.

1. Diagnose student learning
2. Plan a variety of instructional activities to enhance student learning
3. Monitor student learning
4. Maintain high expectations

Diagnose Student Learning

Differentiated instruction calls for multiple modes of assessing student learning, including diagnostic assessment. Students should have multiple options for demonstrating what they already know. This model of planning approaches instruction from a perspective of identifying strengths rather than deficiencies. To implement a diagnosis-based approach to instructional planning, a teacher must have the skill to assess minute to minute, day to day, week to week, and year to year. The purpose of diagnostic assessment is to ascertain, prior to delivery of new content, each student's strengths, weaknesses, knowledge, and skills and to permit the teacher to remediate, accelerate, or differentiate in other appropriate ways the instruction to meet each student's readiness for new learning.

Plan a Variety of Instructional Activities to Enhance Student Learning

Students requiring remedial and supplemental instruction should receive individualized lessons based on learning status and results. In planning, teachers can choose appropriate learning materials and activities for students, depending on their learning outcomes. Also, effective teachers should be aware that without thoughtful planning for real adjustments to instruction (for example, one-to-one tutoring, pull-out special education, reteaching, and any other type of remedial instruction), their students are unlikely to be successful. As a result, struggling students re-experience failure while attempting to learn the same content or skill a second or third time (Chambers, Abrami, Slavin, & Madden, 2011; Lin et al., 2013).

Monitor Student Learning

Building on the diagnosis and implementation of planned learning activities, teachers can evaluate students' learning status to yield informative feedback (formative feedback), which guides instructional decisions focused on areas in need of improvement (Jong et al., 2004).

Maintain High Expectations

Unfortunately, a too frequent experience for students at risk of failing academically is the low expectations of the adults who surround them. Although at-risk students often lack basic skills, teachers must expand their focus beyond what is basic and communicate high expectations. Thus, remedial and supplemental instruction is not necessarily associated with simplistic repeated exposure to prior instruction with low cognitive demand. Rather, effective teachers of struggling students should plan and organize instruction in ways that assist students with mastery of the basic skills while incorporating higher-level learning.

Tables 9.1 and 9.2 (page 94), created by seventh-grade English language arts teacher Jen Morris, show examples of how students can master basic skills while incorporating higher-level learning. Morris administers diagnostic assessments to all her students to determine their reading levels at the beginning of each quarter. Based on the data, she categorizes students into three groups (below, at, and above grade level). This helps her determine where she might focus whole-class instruction and where she needs to implement flexible grouping, therefore differentiating the instruction based on students' abilities (J. Morris, personal communication, August 22, 2014).

Morris reflects on this assessment data as follows.

> At the beginning of each quarter, I administer the district diagnostic assessment to all students to determine their instructional levels in reading. Students must score at least 94 percent in fluency and be within two tenths of a percent in the reading level in order to be considered at that instructional reading level (RL 7 = 6.8–7.8).
>
> I form reading groups based on these results, and I meet with groups four times per week for reading instruction. We use authentic texts so that the level of engagement is higher. I ask students about their reading interests at the beginning of the year. I then find books at their instructional reading levels, and we vote on what to read. We alternate fiction and nonfiction, and we also alternate reading the same book with students reading different texts. I want to give students as much choice as possible in their reading selections, as I know that this is a way to get them more interested and engaged in reading. My reading groups are flexible. This means that as students grow, they are able to move among the reading groups, which, in my view, is an important component of any reading program. This approach improves reading instruction in many ways—flexibility, choice, and engagement. It also leads to solid reading growth in all of my students (except one, and I am working with the special education teacher to devise an individual reading plan for her). (J. Morris, personal communication, August 22, 2014)

Improving Student Self-Efficacy

Many struggling learners have low perceived self-efficacy and negative attribution styles, and they believe that their prior lack of success with learning is due to lack of learning ability. Self-efficacy is a key variable in understanding and promoting student motivation for learning. Self-efficacy influences task choice, effort, resilience, and achievement (Carpenter & Clayton, 2014; Usher, 2009).

Compared with students who do not have confidence in their learning abilities, self-efficacious learners participate more readily, welcome challenges, invest more time and effort, and persist longer when encountering learning blocks. Furthermore, students usually do not engage in learning activities that would lead to negative outcomes (Cheung, 2015; Margolis & McCabe, 2004). Albert Bandura, who first coined the term *self-efficacy* in 1977, states that "people's level of motivation, affective states, and actions are based more on what they believe than on what is objectively the case" (p. 2). Subsequently, various researchers propose a number of instructional principles that are likely to improve self-efficacy (Margolis & McCabe, 2004; Schunk, 1985; Usher & Pajares, 2009).

- **Principle 1: Frequently link new work to recent successes.**
  - Stack the deck for success by matching the instruction to struggling students' achievement and readiness levels through stimulating recall of prerequisite learning, shortening and simplifying work, and limiting the number and length of assignments so students can succeed at moderately challenging tasks if they make enough effort.

Table 9.1: Beginning of Quarter 1—Reading

	Comprehension	Grade Level	Services
Student 1	5.6	Below	Individual Education Plan (IEP)
Student 2	5.7	Below	IEP
Student 3	5.7	Below	IEP
Student 4	6.5	Below	Interventionist
Student 5	6.7	Below	Interventionist
Student 6	7.3	Below	Interventionist
Student 7	7.4	Below	Interventionist
Student 8	7.5	Below	Interventionist
Student 9	7.5	Below	Interventionist
Student 10	8.2	At	
Student 11	8.4	At	
Student 12	8.4	At	
Student 13	8.6	At	
Student 14	8.6	At	
Student 15	8.8	Above	
Student 16	8.9	Above	
Student 17	9.0	Above	

Source: James H. Stronge. Used with permission.

Table 9.2: End of Quarter 1—Reading

	Comprehension	Grade Level	Growth	Services
Student 1	5.6	Below	0	IEP
Student 2	6.2	Below	0.5	IEP
Student 3	6.1	Below	0.4	IEP
Student 4	7.0	Below	0.5	Interventionist
Student 5	7.0	Below	0.3	Interventionist
Student 6	7.8	Below	0.5	Interventionist
Student 7	8.2	Below	0.8	Interventionist
Student 8	8.0	Below	0.5	
Student 9	8.1	Below	0.7	
Student 10	8.5	At	0.3	
Student 11	8.7	At	0.3	
Student 12	8.8	At	0.4	
Student 13	8.9	At	0.3	
Student 14	8.9	At	0.3	
Student 15	9.1	Above	0.3	
Student 16	9.3	Above	0.4	
Student 17	9.2	Above	0.2	

Source: James H. Stronge. Used with permission.

- Link new work to previous successes by explicitly showing how new work resembles those past successes and reminding students of what they did to succeed.

- **Principle 2: Teach students the needed learning strategies.**

  - Explicitly and systematically teach students the strategies that produce success.

  - Sequence materials and tasks from easy to difficult.

  - Model and explain clearly.

  - Provide abundant opportunities for guided practice with task-specific feedback.

- **Principle 3: Reinforce students' effort and encourage persistence.**

  - Design tasks that are challenging but within the struggling learners' abilities, and make sure the tasks are doable if students exert reasonable effort.

  - Provide extrinsic, age-appropriate reinforcers (for example, stickers, small toys, free time), when appropriate, to boost students' interest in the work.

  - When giving reinforcers, accompany them with the rationale of why they are given. Reduce reinforcers when students begin to develop a strong sustaining belief that they can succeed.

- **Principle 4: Encourage students to make facilitative attributions for success.**

  - Teach students to attribute success to controllable factors, such as effort, persistence, and correct strategy choices, rather than to uncontrollable factors such as aptitude or ability, task difficulty, luck, mood, or other people.

- **Principle 5: Help students to establish personally important goals.**

  - Listen to struggling learners to learn about their values, interests, and problems, and link learning to these characteristics.

- Design goals that struggling learners find important and interesting and that pique their curiosity.

- Ask struggling learners to develop short-term, specific, achievable goals that can make an important and significant difference in their lives.

- Teach students to evaluate their own work and chart their successes.

Summary

Differentiating instruction begins with careful planning in which the teacher uses data to inform and drive goal setting and instructional decisions. Through adjustment and alignment, differentiated instruction can help students who struggle with whole-group learning achieve at higher levels individually and in small-group settings. This chapter highlighted some core elements of differentiated planning models and practices of holding high expectations and improving student self-efficacy, which are particularly crucial to students who struggle academically.

To close, we provide several handouts to help teachers in their journey toward planning differentiated instruction for struggling learners.

Although teachers believe in and may be knowledgeable about differentiated instruction, they seldom employ it to maximize student learning. It is often reactive and tangential rather than planned and substantive. Vincent Hawkins (2009) suggests three major reasons why differentiated instruction has failed to become common practice in classrooms: (1) lack of teacher confidence, (2) dilution of teacher efficacy, and (3) inconsistent ongoing professional development and personal perseverance. The handout "Steps for Differentiation" (page 97) synthesizes ideas in the literature on differentiation (for example, Beecher & Sweeny, 2008; Borich, 2011; Tomlinson, 2014) to help teachers plan for differentiated instruction in a more concrete and substantive way.

Teachers play an important role in building student self-efficacy. They can strengthen struggling students' self-efficacy by linking new work to recent successes, teaching needed learning and self-management strategies, reinforcing effort and persistence, teaching students to attribute success or failure in learning to effort or strategy use (rather than innate ability), and helping students identify personally important goals (Margolis & McCabe, 2004). The handout "Differentiated Instruction for Struggling Learners: Self-Assessment" (page 98) can help teachers evaluate their differentiation planning design to determine if it is conducive to enhancing struggling learners' self-efficacy.

Teachers can usually identify whether a student is high or low in self-efficacy in the classroom. Some of the signs of high self-efficacy are investing effort in tasks, persisting on tasks, being willing to take on increasingly challenging tasks, and developing innate interests in academic or learning challenges. Teachers can use the handout "Improving Student Self-Efficacy" (page 99) to evaluate their students' self-efficacy and structure their thinking about how to enhance student self-esteem in learning.

Steps for Differentiation

Domains	Questions I can ask myself	What differentiation would look like	My actions
Content	What do I want my students to know? How do I present the materials so that all students, including struggling students, can learn the content?	Differentiation can take the form of varying modalities in which students gain access to important learning, for example by (1) listening, reading, and doing; (2) presenting content in incremental steps, like rungs on a ladder, resulting in a continuum of skill-building tasks; and (3) offering learners a choice in the complexity of content with which they begin a learning task that matches their current level of understanding and from which every learner can experience academic success.	
Process	What do I want my students to be able to do? How can I integrate basic and higher-level thinking skills?	Differentiation can take the form of flexibility by (1) grouping, varying from the whole class to collaborative groups to small groups to individuals, and (2) providing incentives to learn based on students' individual interests and level of understanding.	
Product	What do I want my students to create? How can I teach students to become more self-directed learners?	Differentiation can take the form of varying assessment methods, such as (1) providing students with a menu of choices, including oral responses, interviews, demonstrations, reenactments, portfolios, and formal tests; (2) keeping each learner challenged at his or her level of understanding with content at or slightly above his or her current level; and (3) allowing students to choose how they express what they know, such as writing a story, drawing a picture, or telling about a real-life experience that involves what is being taught.	

Sources: Adapted from Beecher, M., & Sweeny, S. M. (2008). Closing the achievement gap with curriculum enrichment and differentiation: One school's story. Journal of Advanced Academics, 19(3), 502–530; Borich, G. D. (2011). *Effective teaching methods: Research-based practice (7th ed.). Boston: Pearson; Tomlinson, C. A. (2014). The differentiated classroom: Responding to the needs of all learners (2nd ed.). Alexandria, VA: Association for Supervision and Curriculum Development.*

Differentiated Instruction for Struggling Learners: Self-Assessment

	Strongly Disagree	Disagree	Agree	Strongly Agree
I provide learning tasks that challenge but do not frustrate students.				
I give struggling learners work at their proper levels and communicate expectations of success rather than failure.				
I control task difficulty and make timely adjustments according to students' progress in learning.				
I sequence tasks from easy to difficult and model and explain in a step-by-step fashion.				
I begin learning activities with stimulating recall and applying prerequisite learning and proceed to stacking the tasks for success.				
I use a variety of formative assessments to continuously monitor students' mastery rates.				
I draw on students' recent successes and help students link new learning to their previous successes by explicitly showing and asking them how the new learning resembles previous successful learning.				
I encourage students to identify specific, short-term, realistic learning goals and teach them strategies to evaluate their work and chart their successes.				
I teach students facilitative attributions, attributing success to controllable factors such as effort, persistence, and correct use of strategies.				
I provide students with examples of successful work and communicate expectations clearly about what they will aim to accomplish.				
I persuade students to keep trying and teach them to perceive setbacks as opportunities for learning.				
I explicitly teach students needed learning strategies so they know how to approach tasks.				
I provide task-specific feedback that includes corrective comments and justified praise.				

Source: Adapted from Margolis, H., & McCabe, P. P. (2004). Self-efficacy: A key to improving the motivation of struggling learners. Clearing House: A Journal of Educational Strategies, Issues, and Ideas, 77(6), 241–249.

Improving Student Self-Efficacy

Observe your students and determine if they have any behaviors that demonstrate low self-efficacy.	What might have caused the low self-efficacy?	What should you do to improve students' self-efficacy?
☐ Students act out, refuse to work, or shut down when an activity is difficult.	☐ Lack of successful experiences	☐ Modify task difficulty.
☐ Students give up quickly.	☐ No opportunity for mastery	☐ Capitalize on students' interests.
☐ Students do not have faith in their ability to perform a task.	☐ Lack of encouragement and support	☐ Allow students to make choices.
☐ Students provide responses that are not thoughtful or careless.	☐ High stress or anxiety	☐ Use better motivating strategies.
☐	☐ Competitive learning environment	☐ Give frequent, focused feedback.
☐	☐ Inadequate feedback	☐ Encourage accurate attributions.
☐	☐	☐ Set challenging but achievable learning goals.
☐	☐	☐ Divide learning into manageable segments.
☐	☐	☐ Teach students self-management skills.
☐	☐	☐ Modify instructional strategies.
☐	☐	☐
☐	☐	☐
☐	☐	☐

Chapter 10

Planning for Cross-Disciplinary Instruction

Cross-disciplinary instruction is a valuable addition to any teacher's instructional repertoire. The practice of making connections across subject areas is an effective way to engage students in challenging, integrative, and exploratory learning around personal and social concerns that appeal to them. The integration of disciplines can prompt students to learn to think critically and develop a common core of knowledge necessary for success in the 21st century. Given the value and validity of this instructional strategy, a basic question remains: How do teachers plan for quality cross-disciplinary learning experiences?

Knowing how much additional work is required to design and implement cross-disciplinary instruction, is it worth the effort? In answer, numerous compelling reasons should prompt teachers to consider adding cross-disciplinary instruction to their teaching strategies (Alrøe & Noe, 2014; Case, 1991; Jacobs, 1989).

- The problems and situations that students encounter in real-world settings do not completely organize themselves according to fragmented disciplines or traditional school subjects. Many phenomena in real life cannot be adequately understood solely from one disciplinary perspective. Cross-disciplinary instruction provides real-world applications, hence encouraging transfer of learning.

- Cross-disciplinary instruction expands students' perspectives on school subjects. It encourages them to adopt multiple points of view on issues and promotes higher-level thinking skills. With cross-disciplinary instruction, subjects are no longer rigidly separated, and students can explore how one subject connects with or contributes to an understanding of others, therefore developing a more unified sense of process and content for learning.

- Knowledge is a seamless web of interconnections of heterogeneous areas. Cross-disciplinary instruction enables students to see connections among pieces of information and shapes students' overall approach to learning.

- Efficiency is another reason for integrating content. Teaching two aspects of the curriculum concurrently works as least as well as teaching those aspects in isolation—in terms of time allocated.

What Research Says About Cross-Disciplinary Instruction

Cross-disciplinary instruction is described in a variety of ways in research and practice, including *interdisciplinary, multidisciplinary, transdisciplinary, thematic, curriculum integrated, connected, nested, sequenced, shared, webbed, threaded, immersed, networked, blended, unified, coordinated,* and *fused* (Czerniak, Weber, Sandmann, & Ahern, 1999). Regardless of what term is used, the research on cross-disciplinary instruction is generally positive. For example, one early study investigated the engagement rates of students in a mixed-age classroom of third and fourth graders (Yorks & Follo, 1993). Students' time on task was compared using thematic and traditional instruction. Engagement rates were determined by using an observation form, students' self-perceptions, and teacher reflections. The results indicate that the students' engagement rates are higher during thematic (akin to cross-disciplinary) instruction as compared to traditional instruction.

Jason Wingert et al. (2011) studies students' learning through cross-disciplinary projects focused on food, integrating natural sciences, health sciences, social sciences, and humanities. For example, students measure the content of sodium in vending machine foods (chemistry) and study local food distribution systems (economics, health, and wellness). They also research food sources, policy that shapes how food reaches the marketplace, and nutrition-related health issues to produce professional posters conveying information to a consumer audience. The study finds that the integrative learning augments student learning outcomes and students' sense of civic engagement.

A research review conducted by Charlene Czerniak et al. (1999) finds that cross-disciplinary instruction can produce higher standardized achievement scores and increase student interest toward subject content. Another study investigates the impact of interdisciplinary instruction in science (for example, subjects of physics, chemistry, and biology) and mathematics on students' interests in learning. In this study, a 147-item, Likert-type questionnaire on students' interests was administered to 255 eleventh graders. The results show that upper-secondary students' interest in the subjects of mathematics, physics, chemistry, and biology improve with increased instructional interplay and integration among subjects. The results also indicate that students can transfer interest in one subject to another subject through interdisciplinary instruction (Michelsen & Sriraman, 2009).

Arthur Applebee, Mary Adler, and Sheila Flihan (2007) examined eleven interdisciplinary instructional teams involving 30 teachers and 542 students in New York and California. The teams represent an array of approaches to interdisciplinary instruction, ranging from simple correlation to major reconstrual of the contributing disciplines. *Reconstrual instruction* refers to an advanced level of interdisciplinary teaching in which teachers merge concepts and understanding across disciplines in order to create new content and skills that go beyond disciplinary boundaries.

The study finds that teams engaging in the most reconstrual of traditional content also tend to use instructional approaches that emphasize cognitively engaging instruction, such as asking questions, generating ideas, and conducting extended discussion of significant ideas. However, the study also finds that individual members of teaching teams still vary considerably in teaching style, implying that the effective use of interdisciplinary instruction is contingent on specific contexts and flexibility of teacher implementation.

How to Move From Research to Practice

There are many ways to teach content across different curricular disciplines. This section highlights three specific methods—interdisciplinary concept model, cross-disciplinary units, and thematic units.

Interdisciplinary Concept Model

The interdisciplinary concept model, a seminal foundation work by Heidi Hayes Jacobs and James Borland (1986), can serve as a systematic approach to designing cross-disciplinary instruction. They write, "The central aim of this interdisciplinary model is to bring together the discipline perspectives and focus them on the investigation of a target theme, issue, or problem" (p. 54). They also identify four steps for creating an effective interdisciplinary curriculum.

1. Select a topic or theme around which a curriculum can be developed.

2. Brainstorm associations to deliberately explore the theme from all discipline fields with divergent methods to promote spontaneous and unusual creative responses.

3. Formulate guiding questions for inquiry to serve as a scope and sequence from which a unit of study evolves.

4. Develop activities to address the means for exploring the formulated inquiry questions. Activity design is the nuts and bolts of the unit of study.

A framework to guide the planning of integrated units, such as those suggested by the interdisciplinary concept model, is provided in table 10.1.

Table 10.1: Interdisciplinary Concept Model

Decisions	Questions to Ask	Results
1. Choose a theme.	Is this important for students? Why?	Theme
2. Determine big questions.	What is important for students to know at the end of this unit that informs them for the rest of their lives?	Three or four important big questions toward which every teacher and discipline will teach
3. Determine discipline-specific adaptations of the big questions.	What about these questions can be explained or explored through this discipline? What about this discipline can be explained, explored, or elaborated through these questions?	Discipline-specific adaptations of big questions
4. Create overarching and discipline-specific assessments for big questions that students can demonstrate.	In what ways can students demonstrate their answers to the big questions? What criteria will be used to measure success?	Series of authentic tasks and criteria through which students understand the theme and answer the big questions

Source: Snyder, 2010, pp. 37–38.

Cross-Disciplinary Units

Interdisciplinary configuration is particularly feasible for the curriculum and pedagogy in humanities, such as social studies and English (Applebee et al., 2007). Cross-disciplinary interaction can take a variety of forms. To illustrate, consider the following ideas.

- Art teachers can incorporate history into their instruction of film, photography, visual arts, music, dance, theater, creative writing, and digital arts (Pennisi, 2012).

- Teachers can integrate mathematics and science (for example, physics, chemistry, and biology) to create cross-disciplinary instruction, which research finds to produce better learning outcomes and increase student interest toward subject content (Czerniak et al., 1999; Michelsen & Sriraman, 2009).

- Teachers can target particular skills for integration (for example, proportional thinking in data literacy) through the combination of social studies, mathematics, science, and English / language arts (Vahey et al., 2012).

- Teachers can target a topic or concept (for example, evolution) to integrate social studies with biology.

- Responding to the call for expanding literacy instruction across disciplines, teachers can increase the emphasis on reading, writing, and other literacy objectives in science,

history / social studies, and technical subjects (Robelen, 2012).

Thematic Units

Another useful way to incorporate cross-disciplinary instruction in a classroom is through thematic units. Kenneth Moore (2005) describes the practical aspects of thematic design as follows.

Thematic units offer teaching teams a useful, logical, and flexible way to organize for interdisciplinary / cross-curricular teaching over a block of time. It is a curriculum plan that provides opportunities for more relevant, less fragmented, and more stimulating experiences for students. Thematic units may focus on a specific content area or may be global in nature. For example, in language arts, the focus of a theme may be on realistic fiction, or it may center on a global topic such as conflict. The team plans so that insights and understandings from one discipline, such as science, relate to other disciplines, such as literature and social studies. The planning of thematic units requires the identification of a team of teachers and students and the model to be implemented; the identification of a unit theme, including objectives, activities, and evaluative methods; and sufficient planning time made available for team teachers. (p. 213)

According to Michael Hale and Elizabeth City (2006), themes that best serve cross-disciplinary instruction are those that are tested through time, such as "good and evil, life and death, war and peace, love, faith, betrayal, equality, honor, nature, power, and tragedy" (p. 7). Related to this idea of building thematic units on big ideas, James Beane (1995) suggests that cross-disciplinary instruction begins with "problems, issues, and concerns posed by life itself" (p. 616). He stresses that interdisciplinary instruction must have social meaning and defined multidisciplinary integration with the following four characteristics.

1. It is organized around problems and issues of personal and social significance in the real world.

2. It uses pertinent knowledge in the context of topics without regard for subject lines.

3. It studies a current problem rather than for a test or grade-level outcome.

4. It emphasizes projects and activities with real application of knowledge and problem solving.

If these quality characteristics are to be effectively implemented, they must be addressed in the process of planning for the cross-disciplinary learning experience.

Regardless of the method chosen, teachers must have a practical approach to designing and implementing quality cross-disciplinary instruction. The Consortium for Interdisciplinary Teaching and Learning (1995) outlines the following eight criteria that this kind of instruction should meet in planning and implementation.

1. Maintain the integrity of content drawn from the disciplines by using meaningful connections to sustain students' inquiry between and among these disciplines

2. Foster a learning community in which students and teachers determine together the issues, questions, and strategies for investigation

3. Develop democratic classrooms

4. Provide a variety of opportunities for interaction among diverse learners— for example, discussion, investigation, product development, drama, and online asynchronous communication

5. Respect diversity of thought and culture

6. Teach students to use a wide variety of sources, including primary sources, oral communication, direct observation, and experimentation

7. Use multiple symbol systems as tools to learn and present knowledge

8. Use wide-ranging assessments to evaluate both the process and outcomes of student learning

Cross-disciplinary instruction helps students see real connections between topics they experience in their daily lives and further prepares them for the future.

Summary

Learning has greater value and significance when it is authentic and reflects real life. Many important issues in real life are multifaceted rather than neatly compartmentalized into subject-specific areas. Teachers who plan interdisciplinary instruction tap into the logical connections across content areas and organize learning around themes, issues, questions, and topics. Such instruction is powerful in helping students integrate knowledge and develop sustainable curiosity about learning.

To close, we provide several handouts to help teachers in their journey toward planning for effective cross-disciplinary instruction.

In reviewing both the research and the advocacy literature on cross-disciplinary instruction, Applebee et al. (2007) developed a continuum to describe various ways to implement interdisciplinary learning. The handout "Cross-Disciplinary Instruction Continuum" is built on this concept. Teachers can use this handout to determine which variation is optimal in specific classroom situations.

The handout "Forms of Cross-Disciplinary Instruction" (page 106) includes a template teachers can use for guidance in the planning process for cross-disciplinary instruction. The last component of the template—Level of Integration—illustrates how content areas can be integrated at different levels.

The planning process plays a crucial role in determining if a cross-disciplinary unit or project will be successful with students. The handout "Planning for Cross-Disciplinary Instruction: Self-Assessment" (page 107) can help guide teachers in assessing and evaluating their planning process for cross-disciplinary instruction.

Cross-Disciplinary Instruction Continuum

Cross-Disciplinary Approaches	Related Terms	Characterized by	When would this be applicable to my teaching and why?
Predisciplinary	Integrated, thematic	Every day, common sense knowledge; exploration associations among existing knowledge without using a strong disciplinary frame (Most commonly used in early elementary school)	
Disciplinary	Subject based	Traditional school subject area; academic disciplines; discipline-based concepts	
Correlated	Multidisciplinary, complementary, juxtaposed, parallel, sequenced, thematic, webbed	Discipline-based concepts related to common topics across disciplines (for example, literature may be correlated with history or geography); instructions independent of one another with few explicit connections to illuminate different facets of the shared concept, issue, or problem	
Shared	Thematic, interdisciplinary, integrated, broad field curriculum	Overt concepts overlap across disciplines (for example, the concept of justice in literature and social studies); disciplines mutually supportive; instruction in specific disciplines still independent	
Reconstructured	Synthesized, blended, fused, core curriculum, problem centered, integrated, integrative	Concepts reconstructed across disciplines, eliminating disciplinary boundaries; instruction reconstructed to merge concepts and understanding across disciplines	

Source: Adapted from Applebee, A. N., Adler, M., & Flihan, S. (2007). Interdisciplinary curricula in middle and high school class-rooms: Case studies of approaches to curriculum and instruction. American Educational Research Journal, 44(4), 1002–1039.

Forms of Cross-Disciplinary Instruction

Domains	Breakdown of Components
Scope	Subject areas:
	Topics or concepts:
	Time allotted:
	Prerequisite skills:
	Objectives:
	Knowledge:
	Skills:
	Attitudes and values:
	Resources and materials:
Sequence	Introduction:
	Learning activities:
	Assessment:
Level of Integration	☐ Discipline-specific integration (for example, integrating across mathematics areas or integrating reading with writing)
	☐ Content-specific integration (for example, integrating one mathematics concept and one science concept: measurement with study of dinosaurs)
	☐ Process integration (for example, a skill used in multiple disciplines, such as measurement in science and mathematics)
	☐ Methodological integration (for example, the problem-based learning model or inquiry model in social studies and science: examining how electricity works in physics and how it affected society in social studies)
	☐ Thematic integration (for example, taking a topic, such as climate change, and integrating it with science, mathematics, language arts, and social studies)

Source: Adapted from Davison, D. M., Miller, K. W., & Metheny, D. L. (1995). What does integration of science and mathematics really mean? School Science and Mathematics, 95(5), 226–230.

Planning for Cross-Disciplinary Instruction: Self-Assessment

	Poor	Fair	Good	Very Good
It includes a rationale to explain the importance and relevance of cross-disciplinary learning.				
It has substance and real connections to students' real lives.				
It develops learning objectives to cover the content of learning; objectives cover not just knowledge but also skills and attitudes.				
It creates meaningful interdisciplinary activities; offers a web or chart to specifically identify where the connections across disciplines would occur in learning.				
It provides procedures for learning that are sequential and clearly described; procedures are aligned with identified learning objectives.				
It develops evaluation questions aligned with learning objectives that are able to assess students' higher-order thinking skills of analysis, synthesis, evaluation, or creativity.				
It includes performance-based activities and rubrics/criteria to define specific standards of quality.				
It selects, evaluates, and designs sufficient, varied, and relevant student resources.				
Overall, I not only commit to my own discipline but also value other disciplines and commit to background research to identify strong disciplinary links.				
Overall, the designed learning experiences are truly meaningful and productive in that they bring together multiple disciplinary perspectives and help students to focus on the investigation of a target theme, issue, or problem through connected cross disciplines.				

Chapter 11

Planning for Technology-Integrated Learning

Since the 1980s, we have witnessed the harnessing of instruction to technology. According to Lee Shulman (1986), teachers' expertise in teaching is formulated from the integration of content knowledge with pedagogical knowledge, and this integration is called *pedagogical content knowledge*. Punya Mishra and Matthew Koehler (2006) add technological knowledge to this concept and propose *technological pedagogical content knowledge* (TPACK) to emphasize teachers' expertise in making connections across three domains when integrating technology. Consequently, in dialogues about instruction, there is increasing emphasis on teachers' technological pedagogical content knowledge and an integration of all three key components—technology, pedagogy, and content.

Information literacy and information technology skills are essential for students to effectively function in a 21st century society. Furthermore, it is becoming imperative to integrate teaching information literacy and technology skills into regular curriculum (Chu, Chow, & Tse, 2011). Thus, designing technology-integrated learning is becoming an essential component of teacher effectiveness.

A technology-rich lesson requires that teachers draw on extensive content knowledge to understand how to best use content-related technology resources, pedagogical knowledge, and appropriate methods to manage and organize technology use. Effective integration of technology into the classroom depends on teachers who know how to use technology to meet instructional goals. Exemplary teachers who use technology often have greater personal technology skills, allow for open-ended learning activities, and see technology less as an add-on and more as an integral component of the learning plan (Hattie, 2009).

Most teachers, administrators, and students recognize that information technology tools have a fundamental place in the contemporary classroom. If we want to improve practice in terms of technology integration, we must start by planning for that implementation.

The best way to maximize student learning in a technology-enhanced lesson is to engage in the same thoughtful planning that goes into preparing for any other quality lesson. Perhaps the most important element to consider is coherence between technology integration and student learning. Simply placing a computer in the classroom or even using selected technology tools merely for the sake of using them is wrongheaded. Instead, we must plan for instructional technology with the end in mind, asking, "Does the application of technology positively impact student learning?"

What Research Says About Technology-Integrated Learning

Researchers Rana Tamim, Robert Bernard, Eugene Borokhovski, Philip Abrami, and Richard Schmid (2011) synthesized findings from twenty-five meta-analyses to summarize forty years of research studies addressing the question: Does computer technology use affect student achievement in formal, face-to-face classrooms as compared to classrooms with no technology use? Results indicate that the effect of technology use on learning is heterogeneous (in other words, it can be used in a variety of ways), with a mean effect size of 0.33 (it would increase student percentile scores from 50 to 62). Results also indicate that computer technology-supported instruction has a slightly but significantly higher impact than technology applications used for direct instruction.

John Hattie (2009) reviewed seventy-six meta-analyses on computer-assisted instruction. He finds the average effect size across all studies to be 0.37 (an increase of 16 percentile points). He also concludes that the use of computers is more effective when:

- Diverse teaching strategies are used
- Teacher pretraining in the use of computers as a teaching and learning tool is required
- Multiple opportunities for learning are offered
- The student, not the teacher, is in control of learning
- Peer learning is optimized
- Feedback is optimized

Yuen-Kuang Liao and Yungwei Hao (2008) compare the overall effect sizes for thirty meta-analyses of technology-assisted instruction versus conventional instruction. In terms of students' cognitive achievement, they find 90 percent of the studies indicate that students with technology-enhanced learning perform better than students without it. The overall effect size of the cognitive aspect is 0.41.

Student Learning and Technology Use

Research finds teacher-related factors, such as confidence, attitudes toward technology integration, and willingness to undertake a change, influence the use of technology for student learning (Levin & Wadmany, 2008). When technology is aligned with well-defined learning objectives and integrated into the curriculum, it motivates (Liu, 2005; Williams, Carr, & Clifton, 2006) and engages students (Swan et al., 2006), improves student attitudes toward themselves and toward learning (Sivin-Kachala, Bialo, & Rosso, 2000), and develops students' citizenship and global awareness (Crawford & Kirby, 2008). More specifically, technology has the potential to improve student academic learning in many forms, such as the following.

- Improve scores on standardized tests (Park, Khan, & Petrina, 2009)
- Increase the application and production of knowledge for the real world (Gabric, Hovance, Comstock, & Harnisch, 2006)
- Increase the ability of students to manage learning (Webb, 2005)
- Increase the ability to promote achievement for students with special needs (Puckett, 2006; Williams et al., 2006)
- Increase access to information that promotes knowledge, inquiry, and depth of investigation (Levstik & Barton, 2005; Liu, 2005)

Implications for Classroom Technology Use

Educational technology provides educators with valuable tools to develop and reinforce 21st century skills, including: (1) basic skills such as mathematics and reading; (2) digital-age literacy skills such as technological, cultural, and global awareness; (3) inventive thinking skills such as creativity, problem solving, and higher-order thinking; (4) effective communication and interpersonal skills such as writing, public speaking, teamwork, and collaboration; and (5) productivity skills such as creating high-quality products (CEO Forum on Education and Technology, 2001).

A literature review conducted by James Gulek and Hakan Demirtas (2005) indicates that, compared with their non-computer-using counterparts, students in classrooms that provide computers are engaged in more collaborative work, participate in more project-based learning, gain increased access to information, improve research analysis skills, and spend more time doing homework. Research also demonstrates that students direct their own learning, report a greater reliance on active learning strategies, readily engage in problem solving and critical thinking, and consistently show deeper and more flexible uses of technology than students without computers.

In addition, teachers who apply technology with a constructivist approach feel more empowered and spend less time lecturing, have fewer classroom disruptions, and have more engaged learners. Gulek and Demirtas (2005) also find that one-to-one computing is positively associated with cumulative grade-point averages (GPAs), end-of-course grades, writing test scores, and norm- and criterion-referenced standardized test scores.

How to Move From Research to Practice

In the 1980s, Richard Clark famously argued that technology has no more effect on learning than a grocery truck has on the nutritional value of the produce it brings to market (Tamim et al., 2011). Similarly, Steven Ross, Gary Morrison, and Deborah Lowther (2010) state that educational technology is not homogenous; instead, it is a broad variety of modalities, tools, and strategies for learning. Its effectiveness depends on how well it helps teachers and students achieve the desired goals.

The fundamental understanding is that "educational technologies are only as effective as the curriculums, the pedagogies, and the assessment practices that frame their usage" (Kapitzke, 2006, p. ix). As Brad Hokanson and Simon Hooper (2011) point out, "Merely changing the delivery medium will not improve quality. What must change is the instructional method" (p. 141). Therefore, skilled teachers must value the importance of a student-centered, authentic, and interactive learning environment while using computers and information technology in the classroom.

Categories of Instructional Technology Use

There are at least four categories of classroom technology applications. Each serves a specific purpose in enriching the curriculum (Bitter & Pierson, 2005).

1. Technology as a business resource (for communication and information management)

2. Technology as a subject (when the software or hardware is the focus of learning)

3. Technology as content delivery (when it is perceived as an instructional tool)

4. Technology as a lesson support (when it is in the form of a collection of strategies, from simple to complex, to support learning opportunities)

Before planning to use technology, teachers should consider how specific technologies might extend their ability to teach. Technology can do what traditional approaches cannot—simulate dangerous or distant phenomena, connect multiple media formats to produce a polished learning product, and capture the attention of otherwise unengaged students. Informed teachers enjoy an advantage in better reaching their students with various learning modalities and styles, while ill-informed teachers use technology because they think they are supposed to and are not able to use it to advance learning opportunities for their students.

Guidelines for Planning Technology Integration

Gregory Waddoups (2004) analyzed thirty-four research studies designed to identify the impact of technology integration in teaching and learning on student outcomes. The analysis reveals eleven recurring themes associated with the use of technology to improve student learning. These themes were then synthesized into four principles for integrating technology: (1) teachers, (2) curriculum design, (3) technology design, and (4) ongoing formative evaluations.

Teachers, not technology, are the key to unlocking student potential. A teacher's training in, knowledge of, and attitude toward technology and related skills are central to effective technology integration. Technology is the tool whose master greatly shapes the outcome. In the hands of a poorly trained master, technology is ineffectual, a blunt instrument, or worse.

Curriculum design is critical for successful technology integration. Teachers must reconsider their methods and curricula in order to effectively integrate technology. They must factor in the needs and situations of learners and their ability to make use of technology. Several studies illustrate the importance of pairing inquiry-based instruction with technology to enhance academic achievement (for example, Blake & Gentry, 2012; Ebenezer, Osman, & Devairakkam, 2011).

Technology design largely determines the impact of integration efforts on student achievement. It must be flexible enough to be applied to many settings, deliver rich and timely feedback, and provide students with multiple opportunities to engage with the content.

Finally, ongoing evaluations are necessary for continued improvement in technology integration. There is a wealth of variables to consider in the implementation of any integration program. Successful technology integration demands up-front planning and a focus on program evaluation.

In broad terms, planning for technology-integrated learning opportunities entails determining available technology resources, translating available materials into classroom learning, and developing alternative (and appropriate) assessments to monitor technology-enhanced learning. More specifically, the following seven steps capture the essence of planning for and preparing instructional practices that feature technology integration and focus on student results.

1. Decide what content needs to be taught. Use the state, provincial, or regional standards, school curriculum, or curricular framework developed by professional organizations to determine the content and skills objectives. The scope and sequence of expected learning outcomes should be the primary guide in developing a lesson plan.

2. Determine the best teaching strategies and technology to cover the content and skills. The lesson is greatly enhanced if content and technology are matched with a complimentary teaching strategy.

3. Determine whether technology connections are available. After deciding on the appropriate technology, find out if the computer network or other information technologies are in place, what accounts and passwords must be established, and how equipment, labs, and school support are scheduled.

4. Assess teachers' and students' levels of technology knowledge and use. Investigate in advance the software to be used. Identify how much knowledge and skill are required to accomplish the task or lesson.

5. Design the learning activities. Determine what grouping strategies to use, such as individual work, partners, or teams. Organize the sequence of events in a coherent and progressive manner. Decide what supplemental materials are needed, such as textbooks, worksheets, and so on.

6. Develop an alternative plan in case the technology fails. It is important to plan for unexpected problems and issues. Thus, anticipating these problems helps alleviate them in the unhappy event that they actually occur. There is no substitute for experience in working in technology-enhanced settings.

7. Design the assessment of technology-supported learning. Assessment rubrics and student portfolios are two useful alternative assessment tools for student learning in a technology-integrated lesson. Rubrics allow you to set assessment criteria for items that are subjective, such as visual appeal, presentation,

and interaction. Additionally, if you can share rubrics with students in advance, the students gain a sense of the task criteria and learn what is expected of them. Portfolios are powerful tools in monitoring student growth across time, which cannot be captured with standardized testing. If you can embed both technology and rubrics in portfolio development, portfolios not only are valuable for assessment but also useful learning tools and motivators.

Technology is increasingly deemed as a medium for all kinds of learning rather than an end in itself. Instructional applications of technology are especially powerful in facilitating authentic inquiry learning, as it constantly provides students with information and tools to develop a deeper understanding of the context that gives facts and figures meaning. Each course should have standards representing course-specific learning targets that can be supported by instructional technology (Pahomov, 2014).

The following are examples of learning targets for grade 12 history (American government).

- **Sources:** Students analyze a variety of primary source documents gleaned from technology (such as a digital library) and visual representations of information (such as multimedia).

- **Research:** Students independently use the Internet to locate a variety of sources to incorporate into research-based projects.

- **Perspective:** Students express the impact of perspective or bias in evaluating various political systems.

- **Discussion:** In daily class activities, students communicate their ideas (in class discussion, online forums, small group, and so on) on issues relating to political theory using sources to back up their position.

The following are examples of learning targets for grade 9 science (biochemistry).

- **Inquiry:** Students collaboratively identify a question and design and perform an experiment to answer that question.

- **Research:** Students distinguish between different research methods, scientific principles, and appropriate uses of lab equipment through inquiry assisted by the use of technology.

- **Collaboration:** Students assume a role within a group that incorporates scheduling, peer editing, and negotiation using technologies that allow for online collaboration and communication.

- **Presentation:** Students properly label bibliographies, indicate measurements, recognize data in spreadsheets for export to graphs, and use multimedia to present findings in a clear and engaging way.

Now, let's look at some real-life examples of technology use in classrooms (Blair, 2012; Kent School District, n.d.).

- Instead of beginning a lesson on greenhouse effects by listening to a lecture, an elementary student uses the free activities in Physics Education Technology (PhET) Interactive Simulations (https://phet.colorado.edu), which are developed by the University of Colorado Boulder. The PhET website provides a collection of simulations that feature virtual manipulatives for physics, chemistry, and biology.

- Kindergarteners create image-based movies on recycling and insects.

- First graders use word-processing and drawing applications to create a new imaginary setting for a story or a class book.

- Second graders access the Internet and teacher-reviewed links to help them create a PowerPoint presentation, using a storyboard template, to share information about their community's past and present.

- Third graders develop PowerPoint presentations for *Twice-Told Tales*—projects to investigate and analyze several fairy tales for character, setting, plot, and main idea.

- Fourth graders develop elaborate storybooks on free websites such as Storybird or StoryJumper.

- Fifth graders collaborate to launch a web safety wiki to teach other students worldwide about digital citizenship.

Summary

Technology empowers teachers to create authentic discovery and exploration activities that allow students to develop creativity and problem-solving skills as they display their mastery of content. Technology use can serve as a superficial add-on to instruction to simply make it faster, easier, or more convenient to continue teaching or learning in traditional ways (for example, calculators). However, teachers also can plan to integrate technology in ways that help students learn on different, more meaningful levels (for example, simulations and games) (Maddux & Johnson, 2006). A deeper integration of technology has the potential to contribute more significantly to teaching and lead to higher levels of understanding and retention.

To close, we provide several handouts to help teachers in their journey toward planning for technology integration in the classroom.

If teachers are to plan effectively for a technology-student learning connection, it is essential that the technology applications be curriculum driven (Ross et al., 2010). Simply put, this means teachers must think in terms of what needs to be taught and what learning outcomes are expected. Accordingly, teachers should choose the appropriate technology to enhance the intended outcomes. For example, if the use of technology is merely focused on drill and practice, then the results will be basic skills practice with a likely by-product of a watered-down curriculum. Thus, for instructional technology to fulfill its potential, teachers must think—and plan—thoughtfully and thoroughly about its potential use and results.

The handout "Technology Integration Planning Model" (page 115) is a planning template designed to help teachers plan for aligning learning objectives, instructional strategies, and technology. When planning, they should consider congruency among technology, objectives and instructional strategies, availability, and feasibility in terms of their own and students' technology knowledge and skills.

Developing successful lessons that incorporate the use of technology requires thoughtful planning and attention both to the purpose of the instructional activity and the needs of students. The handout "Planning Technology-Integrated Learning: Self-Assessment" (page 116) provides questions for assessing the planning process. Teachers can use this self-assessment tool to identify what works and what does not work when integrating technology in their classrooms. Education leaders also can adapt the tool to assess teachers' technology use or to facilitate conversations with teachers about using technology in instruction.

Technology plays different roles across subject areas. The handout "Adapting Technology to Your Subject Area" (page 117) offers explanations of research syntheses on the impact and roles of technology in four core subjects. Teachers will select their subject area and write a brief reflection about how the research information changed their perceptions of technology in the classroom and what adjustments they might make to their instructional practices.

Technology Integration Planning Model

Learning Objectives:

Curriculum Standards and Intended Learning Outcomes

Step 1: Unpack the curriculum standards or learning objectives for content, skills, dispositions, or cognitive level (if skills).		Step 2: Choose an appropriate instructional strategy.	Step 3: Examine available technology tools.	Step 4: Design learning activities and procedures.	Step 5: Design alternative activities in case of unforeseeable obstacles with technology.	Step 6: Design assessments.
Indicate the cognitive level if it is a skill.		Possible strategies:	Chosen strategies:			
	Creation					
	Evaluation					
	Analysis					
	Application					
	Comprehension					
	Knowledge					
Content, skills, or dispositions (select one):						
Content, skills, or dispositions (select one):						
Content, skills, or dispositions (select one):						
Content, skills, or dispositions (select one):						

Instructional Planning for Effective Teaching © 2016 J. H. Stronge • solution-tree.com

Visit **go.solution-tree.com/instruction** to download this page.

Planning Technology-Integrated Learning: Self-Assessment

	Strongly Disagree	Disagree	Agree	Strongly Agree
I selected technology that serves the lesson's specific educational goals.				
I clearly identified what students will learn as a result of technology integration.				
I prepared quality materials required by the activities.				
Students know what is expected of them and how they should demonstrate what they have learned.				
I selected technology that increases student motivation to learn and engagement with learning.				
I selected technology that creates authentic opportunities for collaboration and interaction.				
I selected technology that supports the development of communication skills (such as writing or oral presentation).				
I selected technology that supports the development of higher-order thinking such as critical-thinking and problem-solving skills.				
I selected technology that promotes creativity and ingenuity.				
I selected technology that helps move the learning environment from teacher dominated to student centered.				
I selected technology that allows for better differentiation and more student choice.				
I selected technology that provides multisensory stimuli, such as images and sounds, to enrich learning.				

Adapting Technology to Your Subject Area

Instructional Technology and Social Studies

Research shows that thoughtful technology integration can positively impact student learning outcomes in social studies (Journell, 2009), especially in promoting students' critical-thinking skills and problem-solving skills (Açikalin, 2010). One study finds Internet use and accessing information from the web are the most common uses of computers in social studies (Açikalin, 2010). Dennis Beck and Jenni Eno (2012) also find that the most frequently used technology tool in a social studies classroom is website access and creation.

Virtual field trips offer an almost authentic experience for students to interact with certain artifacts, locations, and historical characters (Crawford, Hicks, & Doherty, 2009). Games and simulations also provide an immersive environment (Berson & Berson, 2007; Devlin-Scherer & Sardone, 2010). Teachers can use technology tools to publish students' historical narratives, including wikis, blogs, podcasts, and vodcasts (Beck & Eno, 2012).

In order to achieve the ultimate objective of developing students' civic competence, social studies educators must move away from transmission-oriented teaching (Torrez, 2010) and, instead, use student-centered instruction, focusing on skills in historical literacy, historical empathy, and constructing historical narratives (Levstik & Barton, 2005). The Internet offers digitized primary sources (Tally & Goldenberg, 2005), current facts on politics and events, and multiple perspectives, especially on cultural differences (Journell, 2009). However, interpreting primary sources is a difficult process for students (Friedman & Heafner, 2008), and website information alone does not teach students to become responsible citizens. Instead, teachers must guide students in evaluating, interpreting, and synthesizing information.

Instructional Technology and Language Arts

Research indicates that instructional technology has a positive impact on literacy (Balanskat, Blamire, & Kefala, 2006). For example, one study finds that the use of digital tools in instruction can help middle school students achieve significantly better reading performance (Pearson, Ferdig, Blomeyer, & Moran, 2005). Students who use text-based online discussion also improve their critical argument and debating skills (Walker & Pilkington, 2005). Word processing has proven to have a significant positive impact on student writing. In addition, collaborative writing using emails can motivate students to write together and be more reflective on their writing (Harrison et al., 2002).

In a meta-analysis examining the effects of computers on student writing, Amie Goldberg, Michael Russell, and Abigail Cook (2003) find that students who use computers in learning to write are not only more engaged and motivated in their writing but also produce work that is of greater length and higher quality, especially at the secondary level. Furthermore, Binbin Zheng, Mark Warschauer, and George Farkas (2013) find instantaneous computer-based scoring and feedback and online learning communities (where teachers and students post blogs, comments, files, podcasts, presentations, and other media) are beneficial in improving writing outcomes.

However, not all researchers have reached similar positive conclusions. For example, Carole Torgerson and Diana Elbourne (2002) and Richard Andrews (2004) find computer-based teaching has no measurable or very slight positive effects on improving spelling.

page 1 of 4

Instructional Technology and Science

The four emphasized strands of science learning are: (1) understanding scientific explanation, (2) generating scientific evidence, (3) reflecting on scientific knowledge, and (4) participating productively in science (Campbell & Abd-Hamid, 2013). Appropriate use of digital technology has proven to increase students' content knowledge (Lei & Zhao, 2007; Park et al., 2009) and engage students in scientific inquiry (Ebenezer, Kaya, & Ebenezer, 2011; Hug, Krajcik, & Marx, 2005). Specifically, the applications of technology "provide tools that allow students to visualize complex concepts, perform complicated procedures, use the tools of scientists, employ scientific databases with current information, and research matters of scientific and technological concern" (Gabric et al., 2006, p. 80).

Problem-based learning supported by visual stimulation, virtual labs, and advanced digital tools make learning efficient, more interesting, and empowering. Students are more likely to be aware of what they are learning, acquire the needed information to solve authentic problems, and discover how science can be intriguing and useful (Gupta & Fisher, 2012; Guzey & Roehrig, 2012).

Data from the National Assessment of Educational Progress (NAEP) demonstrate that fourth-, eighth-, and twelfth-grade students whose teachers indicate that they integrate computers into their instruction achieve higher science scores than those students whose teachers do not (O'Sullivan, Lauko, Grigg, Qian, & Zhang, 2003). Webb (2005) summarizes four main areas in science learning that a technology-rich environment affects: cognitive development, real-world experience, self-management, and data collection and presentation. However, in order to integrate technology to facilitate students' inquiring minds, teachers must not only be proficient in both hardware and software involved in the process but also organized in advance planning to secure computer labs or laptop carts (Gabric et al., 2006).

Instructional Technology and Mathematics

Research reports positive relationships between the use of instructional technology and students' mathematics learning (Hamilton, 2007; Li & Ma, 2010). For example, technology integration can help close the achievement gap and promote higher-order thinking skills (Rosen & Beck-Hill, 2012). Technology appears to have more significant effects on the mathematics achievement of students with special needs as compared with general education students. The positive effect is more significant when the technology is used with a constructivist approach to teaching than with a traditional approach. One study finds that teachers who use computers, calculators, and other technological devices in their mathematics instruction can improve students' basic skills in fourth, fifth, sixth, and ninth grades (Hudson, Kadan, Lavin, & Vasquez, 2010).

Additionally, research finds online sites, such as class websites, blogs, or wikis, to be effective platforms for communication among students, teachers, and parents who can discuss mathematics standards, assignments, and projects. Through these online sites, teachers also can provide extra resources to help students explore and solve mathematics problems (Tuttle, 2008). However, research also finds particular technology software or programs do not improve student's mathematics learning (for example, Dynarski et al., 2007). Thus, factors related to specific technology software and programs and their implementation are crucial to their success in the classroom.

Reflections

1. What are your strengths in integrating technology into your instruction?

2. What can you improve in integrating technology into your instruction?

3. What content and skills in your subject could be enhanced by technology?

4. What technologies best fit into your extant instructional strategies? Consider the following seven categories of technology (Pitler, Hubbell, Kuhn, & Malenoski, 2007).
    *   Word-processing applications
    *   Organizing and brainstorming software
    *   Multimedia
    *   Data-collection tools
    *   Web resources
    *   Spreadsheet software
    *   Communication software

    Why?

5. What technologies do you think might enhance student learning but also require you to restructure your instructional model?

Sources: Açikalin, M. (2010, October). Exemplary social studies teachers use of computer-supported instruction in the classroom. The Turkish Online Journal of Educational Technology, 9*(4), 66–82; Andrews, R. (Ed.). (2004).* The impact of ICT on literacy education. *New York: RoutledgeFalmer; Balanskat, A., Blamire, R., & Kefala, S. (2006, December).* The ICT impact report: A review of studies of ICT impact on schools in Europe. *Brussels, Belgium: European Schoolnet; Beck, D., & Eno, J. (2012). Signature pedagogy: A literature review of social studies and technology research.* Computers in the Schools, 29*(1–2), 70–94; Berson, I. R., & Berson,*

M. J. (2007). *Exploring complex social phenomena with computer simulations.* Social Education, 71(3), 136–139; Campbell, T., & Abd-Hamid, N. H. (2013). *Technology use in science instruction (TUSI): Aligning the integration of technology in science instruction in ways supportive of science education reform.* Journal of Science Education and Technology, 22(4), 572–588; Crawford, B., Hicks, D., & Doherty, N. (2009). *Worth the WAIT: Engaging social studies students with art in a digital age.* Social Education, 73(3), 136–139; Devlin-Scherer, R., & Sardone, N. B. (2010). *Digital simulation games for social studies classrooms.* Clearing House: A Journal of Educational Strategies, Issues, and Ideas, 83(4), 138–144; Ebenezer, J., Kaya, O. N., & Ebenezer, D. L. (2011). *Engaging students in environmental research projects: Perceptions of fluency with innovative technologies and levels of scientific inquiry abilities.* Journal of Research in Science Teaching, 48(1), 94–116; Friedman, A. M., & Heafner, T. L. (2008). *Finding and contextualizing resources: A digital literacy tool's impact in ninth-grade world history.* Clearing House: A Journal of Educational Strategies, Issues, and Ideas, 82(2), 82–86; Gabric, K. M., Hovance, C. Z., Comstock, S. L., & Harnisch, D. L. (2006). *Scientists in their own classroom: The use of Type II technology in the science classroom.* Computers in the Schools, 22(3–4), 77–91; Goldberg, A., Russell, M., & Cook, A. (2003). *The effect of computers on student writing: A meta-analysis of studies from 1992 to 2002.* Journal of Technology, Learning, and Assessment, 2(1), 1–51. Accessed at https:// ejournals.bc.edu/ojs/index.php/jtla/article/viewFile/1661/1503 on April 30, 2015; Gupta, A., & Fisher, D. (2012). *Technology-supported learning environments in science classrooms in India.* Learning Environments Research, 15(2), 195–216; Guzey, S., & Roehrig, G. (2012). *Educational technology in a novice science teachers' classroom.* In I. L. Chen & D. McPheeters (Eds.), Cases on educational technology integration in urban schools (pp. 145–153). Hershey, PA: IGI Global; Hamilton, B. (2007). *It's elementary! Integrating technology in the primary grades.* Eugene, OR: International Society for Technology in Education; Harrison, C., Comber, C., Fisher, T., Haw, K., Lewin, C., Lunzer, E., et al. (2002). *ImpaCT2: The impact of information and communication technologies on pupil learning and attainment.* Coventry, England: British Educational Communications and Technology Agency; Hudson, S., Kadan, S., Lavin, K., & Vasquez, T. (2010). *Improving basic math skills using technology.* Action research project, Saint Xavier University, Chicago; Hug, B., Krajcik, J. S., & Marx, R. W. (2005). *Using innovative learning technologies to promote learning and engagement in an urban science classroom.* Urban Education, 40(4), 446–472; Lei, J., & Zhao, Y. (2007). *Technology uses and student achievement: A longitudinal study.* Computers and Education, 49(2), 284–296; Levstik, L. S., & Barton, K. C. (2005). Doing history: Investigating with children in elementary and middle schools (3rd ed.). Mahwah, NJ: Erlbaum; Li, Q., & Ma, X. (2010). *A meta-analysis of the effects of computer technology on school students' mathematics learning.* Educational Psychology Review, 22(3), 215–243; Journell, W. (2009). *Maximizing the potential of computer-based technology in secondary social studies education.* Social Studies Research and Practice, 4(1), 56–70; O'Sullivan, C. Y., Lauko, M. A., Grigg, W. S., Qian, J., & Zhang, J. (2003, January). *The nation's report card: Science 2000 (NCES 2003–453).* Washington, DC: U.S. Department of Education, Institute of Education Science, National Center for Education Statistics; Park, H., Khan, S., & Petrina, S. (2009). *ICT in science education: A quasi-experimental study of achievement, attitudes toward science, and career aspirations of Korean middle school students.* International Journal of Science Education, 31(8), 993–1012; Pearson, P. D., Ferdig, R. E., Blomeyer, R. L., Jr., & Moran, J. (2005, November). *The effects of technology on reading performance in the middle-school grades: A meta-analysis with recommendations for policy.* Naperville, IL: Learning Point Associates; Rosen, Y., & Beck-Hill, D. (2012). *Intertwining digital content and a one-to-one laptop environment in teaching and learning: Lessons from the time to know program.* Journal of Research on Technology in Education, 44(3), 225–241; Tally, B., & Goldenberg, L. B. (2005). *Fostering historical thinking with digitized primary sources.* Journal of Research on Technology in Education, 38(1), 1–21; Torgerson, C. J., & Elbourne, D. (2002). *A systematic review and meta-analysis of the effectiveness of information and communication technology (ICT) on the teaching of spelling.* Journal of Research in Reading, 25(2), 129–143; Torrez, C. F., & Waring, S. M. (2009). *Elementary school students, artifacts and primary sources: Learning to engage in historical inquiry.* Social Studies Research and Practice, 4(2), 79–86; Tuttle, H. G. (2008). *Technology = math success.* Technology and Learning, 28(7), 30; Walker, A., & Pilkington, R. M. (2005). *Using computers to assist in developing key literacy skills.* In M. Monteith (Ed.), Teaching secondary school literacies (pp. 71–96). New York: McGraw-Hill; Webb, M. E. (2005). *Affordances of ICT in science learning: Implications for an integrated pedagogy.* International Journal of Science Education, 27(6), 705–735; Zheng, B., Warschauer, M., & Farkas, G. (2013). *Digital writing and diversity: The effects of school laptop programs on literacy processes and outcomes.* Journal of Educational Computing Research, 48(3), 267–299.

Chapter 12
Team Planning

For too long, teaching was practiced in isolation. The teacher would enter the classroom, shut the door, and teach. Other than incidental interactions with colleagues—for example, before and after school, during lunch, and in the occasional meeting—teachers were almost independent agents. Fortunately, this paradigm of isolation has begun to give way to more collaborative and shared teaching practices.

An essential aspect of collaborative work for teachers is team planning. Instruction is not only the time teachers spend interacting with students in the classroom; it is also the time spent away from students engaging in planning activities such as learning, collaborative inquiry, communicating, and problem solving. Common planning should be structured, ongoing, sustained, and supported. We've known for a long time that the lack of opportunity to discuss plans with others prevents teachers from examining their practice and deliberating about issues to improve teaching and learning (McCutcheon, 1980). Team planning allows teachers to collaboratively examine important issues and develop a collective approach to instruction (Jackson & Davis, 2000). Additionally, teachers who collaborate share resources and decision-making responsibilities; they also hold joint expectations for achieving common goals (Carter, Prater, Jackson, & Marchant, 2009; Cook & Faulkner, 2010).

What Research Says About Team Planning

Valeri Helterbran (2008) points out that "planning, an invisible and solitary part of teaching, has changed little over time . . . Despite the inherent logic behind and benefits of planning with others, collaborative planning seems not to have taken root in many schools" (p. 90). However, extant research is replete with examples of how team planning impacts teacher effectiveness. One study finds that teachers who are engaged in collaborative planning, teaching, observing, revising, and reteaching lessons can increase their knowledge of subject matter, increase knowledge of instruction, increase the ability to observe students, build stronger collegial networks, enhance the connection of daily practice to long-term goals, maintain stronger motivation and sense of efficacy, and improve the quality of lesson plans (Lewis, Perry, & Hurd, 2004). Taken collectively, these benefits provide a powerful endorsement for team planning.

Research also finds that teachers who invest more time in planning are more likely to develop thought-provoking lessons. Kerri Lookabill (2008) finds that teachers who plan longer, either individually or collaboratively, use a larger variety of research-based instructional strategies. In particular, these teachers reflect on previous lessons in order to make improvements for subsequent lessons.

Research also indicates that collaboration can improve the quality of lesson plans as measured by the following criteria (Carter et al., 2009; Cook & Faulkner, 2010; Lewis, Perry, & Hurd, 2004).

- Specifying or selecting learning objectives for students
- Specifying or selecting procedures for lessons
- Specifying or selecting content materials and media for lessons
- Specifying or selecting materials and procedures for assessing learner progress
- Using information about students to plan and organize instruction to accommodate

differences in developmental and individual needs

- Using knowledge of students' needs, interests, and experiences

- Incorporating multiculturalism and diversity in lessons

Collaborative planning is essential to teacher teams for interdisciplinary instruction because it can provide time for teachers to discuss students' developmental needs, create a sense of collegial support, and design developmentally appropriate instructional activities. In a study of collaborative planning, teachers on interdisciplinary teams who had common planning time reported significantly higher levels of personal efficacy and more positive perceptions of their working environment than those on interdisciplinary teams who did not have common planning time or were departmentalized (Rimpola, 2014; Warren & Payne, 1997).

In addition, collaborative planning in content areas between special education teachers and general education teachers is considered essential for the success of students with special needs. Through collaboration, special education, and general education teachers can bring their respective expertise about content knowledge and instruction into the planning procedures of selecting and organizing content, determining activities, identifying accommodations and modifications, and assessing student performance (Jitendra, Edwards, Choutka, & Treadway, 2002).

After several years of working with school districts and witnessing the ineffective results of various large-scale, whole-school reform efforts, Roger Stewart and Jonathan Brendefur (2005) conclude that the best way to bring about positive change at the classroom level is to adopt a model wherein small groups of teachers work in collaborative learning communities focused on improving day-to-day instruction. Small groups of teachers who work collaboratively on relatively short-term goals can make schools and classrooms work better for students (Schmoker, 2004).

How to Move From Research to Practice

Without a doubt, team planning is valuable. Teachers need time to share ideas about teaching and learning,

student progress, and student outcomes. Furthermore, team planning can reduce duplicating efforts or the probability of leaving out important content. It can increase planning time for designing enrichment activities and facilitate coordination efforts across disciplines. The English teacher and the history teacher, for example, could design their courses to cover the same time periods simultaneously. This gives students the opportunity to see the connections between the two disciplines (Moore, 2005).

Another option is to collaborate across grades in the same subjects. For example, elementary teachers can work together as grade-level teams to develop lessons. Thus, opportunities for teachers to engage in critical thinking are greatly enhanced through team planning. The following list summarizes several benefits of collaboration (Goddard, Goddard, & Tschannen-Moran, 2007; Levine & Marcus, 2010; Meirink, Imants, Meijer, & Verloop, 2010; Moolenaar et al., 2012).

- Broadening teaching skills and enhancing commitment to continuous improvement

- Gaining new and current ideas and materials

- Enhancing teacher morale due to reduced isolation

- Developing a curriculum that is more horizontally and vertically coherent

- Sharing knowledge on how to reach diverse student populations

- Increasing self-efficacy and collective efficacy

- Enhancing the willingness to experiment and take risks

Steven Mertens, Nancy Flowers, Vincent Anfara, and Micki Caskey (2010) identify a number of principles that teams should consider so that common planning time can enhance practice and foster collegiality among teachers. Common planning time should:

- Have a clearly defined purpose and expectations for how it will be used

- Focus on improving teaching skills, which includes discussing instruction and specific strategies used in daily practice

- Lead to the accomplishment of a target goal or a tangible product, such as a team unit, writing prompt, or assessment tools, to positively affect student learning

- Engage an instructional leader to facilitate meetings and increase the focus on teaching and learning

Lesson Study

A number of educators have suggested adopting lesson study as a form of collaborative planning and professional development (Fernandez, 2005; Lewis et al., 2004; Lewis & Tsuchida, 1998; Stewart & Brendefur, 2005; Stigler & Hiebert, 1999). Within the lesson study model, a collaborative group of teachers engages in a recursive cycle to study curriculum, formulate learning objectives, plan a lesson, observe the teaching of the lesson, and discuss and revise the plan and instruction. Conducting a lesson study usually comprises the following five steps (Fernandez, 2002; Lewis et al., 2004; Lewis, Perry, & Murata, 2006).

1. A group of teachers meets to study the curriculum and standards and consider long-term goals for student learning and development. Group members identify a learning goal for their students and relevant instructional strategies that might lead to the achievement of that goal.

2. The teachers develop a meticulously written lesson plan as a group. The plan describes in detail the design of the lesson, including elements such as how the lesson is related to the curriculum and long-term goals, steps in the lesson, expected student reactions or responses, teacher responses to student reactions, and methods of evaluating the lesson's success.

3. One of the teachers in the group teaches the lesson to his or her students. The other group members observe the lesson and take careful notes, usually on an overlay of the lesson plan.

4. After observing the lesson, the group reconvenes to discuss the lesson delivery. This meeting involves rich conversation about what went well during the lesson and what did not turn out as planned. The group then revises the lesson plan based on the feedback.

5. The other team members teach the revised lesson. Teachers who do not have the opportunity to reteach the lesson in its revised form—because they have to keep moving along with their curricula—teach the lesson the following school year.

Powerful cases of teacher collaboration similar to lesson study also can be found in China. Chinese teachers, even at the primary level, are organized into teacher research groups, in which all members teach the same subject. Teachers share office workspace, schedule common planning and meeting times, and have rich opportunities for interaction. Each teacher research group is led by a teacher identified as one of the best in that subject. With a focus on improving their practices, group members discuss ways to teach the subject, observe one another in class, organize in-service education, and mentor new and preservice teachers. The groups meet after students complete their exams to determine areas in need of improvement and how to improve them. Novice teachers teach public lessons, which are critiqued by their colleagues (Preus, 2007).

Over the years, a number of teacher-development practices have emerged in China, many of which have become standard practice. One of the most important lessons learned from these teachers is the focus on collaboration and lesson peer review. Although some United States teachers discuss the value of spending time in other teachers' classrooms, it is not pervasive as a technique for professional growth and change (Grant et al., 2014).

There is one striking difference between teachers in China and the United States—the teachers in China improve their teaching through lesson research, or cycles of activities in which teachers group by subject and grade level to design, implement, observe, and critique lessons together (Tsui & Wong, 2009). Another format of in-service professional development is open lessons, which are exemplary demonstration lessons presented by expert teachers from within the local district, from a different area in the province, or from a different province altogether (Tsui & Wong, 2009).

Whole-Faculty Study Groups

Another useful form of organizing collaborative planning is Murphy's whole-faculty study groups model (Murphy & Lick, 2005). In this model, all faculty members participate in study groups with no more than six members. The study groups facilitate learning new theories, observe demonstrations, and practice new models of teaching (for example, concept attainment, inductive thinking, and cooperative learning). Groups meet weekly for an hour to identify the goals of student learning, plan and practice lessons using the teaching models, and regularly make and critique videotapes of their teaching. Leadership in the groups is shared and rotated among group members.

Summary

Team planning engages teachers in sharing their knowledge and challenges, solving problems collaboratively, and giving and receiving support within a learning community. However, flexible scheduling to allow teachers more common planning time does not automatically transform instructional teams into high-performing learning organizations. It takes will, practice, and time to turn the shared time of planning into meaningful experiences, which can truly translate into better integrated learning opportunities for students.

To close, we provide several handouts to help teachers in their journey toward planning for effective collaborative teams.

As teacher teams engage in collaborative planning, it is important for teams to set specific goals. For example, participating teachers can identify a particular concern within teaching and learning that they want to explore. The handout "Collaborative Planning: Self-Assessment" is a self-assessment tool designed to facilitate teacher reflection on the collaborative planning experience. The statements on this handout can be used for reflection or evaluation of the quality of shared planning time.

With increasing classroom inclusiveness and the popularity of co-teaching, a greater need has emerged for cooperation and communication among general and special education teachers working together as a team. The handout "Collaborative Planning Between General and Special Education Teachers" (page 126) can help facilitate the process of such collaborative planning. It is designed to encourage collegial exchanges of strategies and increase understanding of all students' needs. This handout is based on Jeanne Schumm et al.'s (1995) flow of the planning process model and includes preplanning, interactive planning, and postplanning activities.

Teachers often find themselves perceived by the public as working short hours and only being on the job when they are directly engaged with students in the classroom. Mary Kennedy (2010) finds that a typical teacher in the United States spends a vast majority of time engaged in instructional delivery. Teachers are typically allocated one hour to plan and about five hours to teach each day. Thus, the official ratio of planning time to instructional time is about 1:5. In other words, about ten to twelve minutes are available to plan for an hour's instruction. However, in countries such as China, the ratio of planning time to instructional time is about 2:1, and teachers typically have two hours to plan for an hour's teaching. The handout "Time Management" (page 127) is designed to help teachers reflect on how their time at school is cut and sliced and for what purposes, thus raising awareness of how time for individual and collaborative planning is used.

Collaborative Planning: Self-Assessment

	Agree Strongly	Agree	Disagree	Disagree Strongly
We improved collegiality.				
We created networks for developing action plans geared toward better performance.				
We increased the feeling of self-efficacy in teaching.				
We improved the faculty's ability to foster student achievement.				
We discussed and solved specific problems that arise in day-to-day instruction.				
We collaborated on mutual goals and shared responsibility in decision making.				
We monitored the impact of instructional initiatives on student learning.				
We opened discussion around pedagogical knowledge.				
We provided opportunities for reflection and shared critique/feedback of practice.				
We promoted the ideas of shared accountability and shared instructional practices.				
We expanded our understanding of the curriculum, pedagogy, and the needs of our students.				
We ensured that all team members have a reasonable level of ownership in the collaborative process.				

Benefits of collaboration:

Barriers to collaboration:

Collaborative Planning Between General and Special Education Teachers

Preplanning involves preparing a lesson or a set of learning experiences: gathering and reading relevant background materials, thinking through procedures and grouping, and considering factors that can enhance learning. Preplanning also includes writing objectives, outlining procedures, and specifying desired outcomes and evaluation plans.

↓

Interactive planning involves monitoring plan implementation and making adaptations in response to student progress. It is often concurrent with teaching, making adjustments on an incidental basis during ongoing instruction.

↓

Postplanning involves planning for the next lesson or projecting for the next unit or even the next year. This is follow-up planning. Incorporate student reactions (including their performance on assignments and tests) into postplanning, and use this information to inform and guide upcoming lessons.

We will use this cycle of collaborative planning (please select one):

☐ Daily   ☐ Unit

☐ Weekly   ☐ Long Term

Notes:

Preplanning: Actions Taken

☐ Design agenda (sequence, activities)
☐ Set goals/objectives
☐ Determine information sources and materials
☐ Design assessment
☐ Plan the physical environment and grouping
☐ Identify adaptations (for example, academic or social)

Interactive Planning: Actions Taken

☐ Adjust level of adherence to the written plan
☐ Monitor student understanding and behavior
☐ Make adaptations

Postplanning: Actions Taken

☐ Develop immediate plans
☐ Develop plans for next year
☐ Revise plans

Source: Adapted from Schumm, J. S., Vaughn, S., Haager, D., McDowell, J., Rothlein, L., & Saumell, L. (1995). General education teacher planning: What can students with learning disabilities expect? Exceptional Children, 61(4), 335–352.

Instructional Planning for Effective Teaching © 2016 Solution Tree Press • solution-tree.com

Visit **go.solution-tree.com/instruction** to download this page.

Time Management

	Monday	Tuesday	Wednesday	Thursday	Friday	Saturday	Sunday
7 a.m.							
8 a.m.							
9 a.m.							
10 a.m.							
11 a.m.							
12 p.m.							
1 p.m.							
2 p.m.							
3 p.m.							
4 p.m.							
5 p.m.							
6 p.m.							
7 p.m.							

Total number of working hours per week: _____

Time typically designated to the following activities:

Instruction:	Grading:	Staff meetings:
Parent meetings:	Professional development:	Individual planning:
Collaborative planning:	Administrative duties (such as writing reports):	Others:

Reflection

What strategies can you and your colleagues use to ensure significant chunks of time are available during the school week to conduct collaborative planning? Can you schedule more creatively and make periods of time more collaborative and functional? (For example, can you put together two planning periods or organize fragmented planning time to create a longer block of time for sustained collaborative planning?)

References and Resources

Açikalin, M. (2010, October). Exemplary social studies teachers use of computer-supported instruction in the classroom. *The Turkish Online Journal of Educational Technology, 9*(4), 66–82.

Akhlaq, M., Chudhary, M. A., Malik, S., ul-Hassan, S., & Mehmood, K. (2010). An experimental study to assess the motivational techniques used by teachers in the teaching of chemistry. *Journal of Education and Sociology, 3*, 36–52.

Allington, R. L., & Johnston, P. H. (2000). *What do we know about effective fourth-grade teachers and their classrooms?* (Report Series 13010). Albany: National Research Center on English Learning and Achievement, State University of New York.

Alrøe, H. F., & Noe, E. (2014). Second-order science of interdisciplinary research: A polyocular framework for wicked problems. *Constructivist Foundations, 10*(1), 65–76.

Anderson, L. W., & Krathwohl, D. R. (Eds.). (2001). *A taxonomy for learning, teaching, and assessing: A revision of Bloom's taxonomy of educational objectives.* New York: Longman.

Andrews, R. (Ed.). (2004). *The impact of ICT on literacy education.* New York: RoutledgeFalmer.

Applebee, A. N., Adler, M., & Flihan, S. (2007). Interdisciplinary curricula in middle and high school classrooms: Case studies of approaches to curriculum and instruction. *American Educational Research Journal, 44*(4), 1002–1039.

Ark, T. V., & Schneider, C. (2014). *Deeper learning for every student every day.* Menlo Park, CA: Hewlett Foundation. Accessed at www.hewlett.org/sites/default/files/Deeper%20Learning%20for%20Every %20Student%20EVery%20Day_GETTING%20SMART_1.2014.pdf on April 30, 2015.

Ausubel, D. (1978). In defense of advance organizers: A reply to the critics. *Review of Educational Research, 48*(2), 251–257.

Authentic Learning. (n.d.). *About authentic learning.* Accessed at http://authenticlearning.info/AuthenticLearning /Home.html on April 30, 2015.

Baartman, L. K. J., & de Bruijn, E. (2011). Integrating knowledge, skills, and attitudes: Conceptualising learning processes towards vocational competence. *Educational Research Review, 6*(2), 125–134.

Balanskat, A., Blamire, R., & Kefala, S. (2006, December). *The ICT impact report: A review of studies of ICT impact on schools in Europe.* Brussels, Belgium: European Schoolnet.

Bandura, A. (1997). Exercise of personal and collective efficacy in changing societies. In A. Bandura (Ed.), *Self-efficacy in changing societies* (pp. 1–45). New York: Cambridge University Press.

Beane, J. A. (1995). Curriculum integration and the disciplines of knowledge. *Phi Delta Kappan, 76*(8), 616–622.

Beck, D., & Eno, J. (2012). Signature pedagogy: A literature review of social studies and technology research. *Computers in the Schools, 29*(1–2), 70–94.

Beecher, M., & Sweeny, S. M. (2008). Closing the achievement gap with curriculum enrichment and differentiation: One school's story. *Journal of Advanced Academics, 19*(3), 502–530.

Berson, I. R., & Berson, M. J. (2007). Exploring complex social phenomena with computer simulations. *Social Education, 71*(3), 136–139.

Bitter, G. G., & Pierson, M. E. (2005). *Using technology in the classroom* (6th ed.). Boston: Pearson.

Black, P., & Wiliam, D. (1998). Assessment and classroom learning. *Assessment in Education: Principles, Policy, and Practice, 5*(1), 7–74.

Blair, N. (2012). Technology integration for the "new" 21st century learners. *Principal, 91*(3), 8–11. Accessed at www.naesp.org/sites/default/files/Blair_JF12.pdf on April 30, 2015.

Blake, S., & Gentry, A. R. (2012). Inquiry and technology. In S. Blake, D. L. Winsor, & L. Allen (Eds.), *Child development and the use of technology: Perspectives, applications, and experiences* (pp. 169–193). Hershey, PA: IGI Global.

Bongiorno, D. (Ed.). (2011). *Student assessment: Using student achievement data to support instructional decision making* [White paper]. Alexandria, VA: National Association of Elementary School Principals. Accessed at www.naesp.org/sites/default/files/Student%20Achievement_blue.pdf on April 30, 2015.

Borich, G. D. (2011). *Effective teaching methods: Research-based practice* (7th ed.). Boston: Pearson.

Branch, R. M., Kim, D., & Koenecke, L. (1999). *Evaluating online educational materials for use in instruction.* Accessed at http://files.eric.ed.gov/fulltext/ED430564.pdf on April 30, 2015. (ED430564)

Brody, L. E., & Benbow, C. P. (1987). Accelerative strategies: How effective are they for the gifted? *Gifted Child Quarterly, 31*(3), 105–110.

Brupbacher, L., & Wilson, D. (2008). When TEASing is a good thing. *TechEdge, 28*(2), 38–39.

Buttram, J. L., & Waters, T. (1997). Improving America's schools through standards-based education. *NASSP Bulletin, 81*(590), 1–6.

Campbell, T., & Abd-Hamid, N. H. (2013). Technology use in science instruction (TUSI): Aligning the integration of technology in science instruction in ways supportive of science education reform. *Journal of Science Education and Technology, 22*(4), 572–588.

Carpenter, D. M., II, & Clayton, G. (2014). Measuring the relationship between self-efficacy and math performance among first-generation college-bound middle school students. *Middle Grades Research Journal, 9*(2), 109–126.

Carter, N., Prater, M. A., Jackson, A., & Marchant, M. (2009). Educators' perceptions of collaborative planning processes for students with disabilities. *Preventing School Failure, 54*(1), 60–70.

Case, R. (1991). The anatomy of curricular integration. *Canadian Journal of Education, 16*(2), 215–224.

Cavanaugh, R. A., Heward, W. L., & Donelson, F. (1996). Effects of response cards during lesson closure on the academic performance of secondary students in an earth science course. *Journal of Applied Behavior Analysis, 29*(3), 403–406.

CEO Forum on Education and Technology. (2001, June). *The CEO Forum school technology and readiness report: Key building blocks for student achievement in the 21st century.* Washington, DC: Author. Accessed at http://schoolnet.org.za/CoL/ACE/course/ukzncore1b/documents/core1b_CEO_Forum_Report4.pdf on April 30, 2015.

Chambers, B., Abrami, P. C., Slavin, R. E., & Madden, N. A. (2011). A three-tier model of reading instruction supported by technology. *International Journal of Innovation and Learning, 9*(3), 286–297.

Chan, Y., Hui, D., Dickinson, A. R., Chu, D., Cheng, D., Cheung, E., et al. (2010). Engineering outreach: A successful initiative with gifted students in science and technology in Hong Kong. *IEEE Transactions, 53*(1), 158–171.

Cheung, D. (2015). The combined effects of classroom teaching and learning strategy use on students' chemistry self-efficacy. *Research in Science Education, 45*(1), 101–116.

Chu, S. K. W., Chow, K., & Tse, S. K. (2011). Using collaborative teaching and inquiry project-based learning to help primary school students develop information literacy and information skills. *Library and Information Science Research, 33*(2), 132–143.

Cook, C. M., & Faulkner, S. A. (2010). The use of common planning time: A case study of two Kentucky schools to watch. *Research in Middle Level Education Online, 34*(2), 1–12.

Consortium for Interdisciplinary Teaching and Learning. (1995). *Position statement on interdisciplinary learning, pre–K to grade 4.* Accessed at www.ncte.org/positions/statements/interdisclearnprek4 on August 21, 2015.

Cotton, K. (2000). *The schooling practices that matter most.* Portland, OR: Northwest Regional Educational Laboratory.

Covey, S. R. (1989). *The 7 habits of highly effective people: Powerful lessons in personal change.* New York: Simon & Schuster.

Crawford, B., Hicks, D., & Doherty, N. (2009). Worth the WAIT: Engaging social studies students with art in a digital age. *Social Education, 73*(3), 136–139.

Crawford, E. O., & Kirby, M. M. (2008). Fostering students' global awareness: Technology applications in social studies teaching and learning. *Journal of Curriculum and Instruction, 2*(1), 56–73. Accessed at www.joci.ecu.edu/index.php/JoCI/article/view/12 on April 30, 2015.

Crooks, T. J. (1988). The impact of classroom evaluation practices on students. *Review of Educational Research, 58*(4), 438–481.

Csikszentmihalyi, M., Rathunde, K., & Whalen, S. (1993). *Talented teenagers: The roots of success and failure.* New York: Cambridge University Press.

Czerniak, C. M., Weber, W. B., Jr., Sandmann, A., & Ahern, J. (1999). A literature review of science and mathematics integration. *School Science and Mathematics, 99*(8), 421–430.

Danielson, C. (2007). *Enhancing professional practice: A framework for teaching* (2nd ed.). Alexandria, VA: Association for Supervision and Curriculum Development.

Davison, D. M., Miller, K. W., & Metheny, D. L. (1995). What does integration of science and mathematics really mean? *School Science and Mathematics, 95*(5), 226–230.

Dell'Olio, J. M., & Donk, T. (2007). *Models of teaching: Connecting student learning with standards.* Thousand Oaks, CA: SAGE.

Devlin-Scherer, R., & Sardone, N. B. (2010). Digital simulation games for social studies classrooms. *Clearing House: A Journal of Educational Strategies, Issues, and Ideas, 83*(4), 138–144.

Doherty, E., & Evans, L. (1981). Independent study process: They can think, can't they? *Journal for the Education of the Gifted, 4*(1), 106–111.

Duchastel, P. C., & Merrill, P. F. (1973). The effects of behavioral objectives on learning: A review of empirical studies. *Review of Educational Research, 43*(1), 53–69.

Duffy, H. (2007). *Meeting the needs of significantly struggling learners in high school: A look at approaches to tiered intervention.* Accessed at http://files.eric.ed.gov/fulltext/ED501084.pdf on April 30, 2015. (ED501084)

Dynarski, M., Agodini, R., Heaviside, S., Novak, T., Carey, N., Campuzano, L., et al. (2007, March). *Effectiveness of reading and mathematics software products: Findings from the first student cohort* (NCEE 2007-4005). Washington, DC: U.S. Department of Education, Institute of Education Sciences.

Ebenezer, J., Kaya, O. N., & Ebenezer, D. L. (2011). Engaging students in environmental research projects: Perceptions of fluency with innovative technologies and levels of scientific inquiry abilities. *Journal of Research in Science Teaching, 48*(1), 94–116.

Ebenezer, J., Osman, N. K., & Devairakkam, L. (2011) Engaging students in environmental research projects: Perceptions of fluency with innovative technologies and levels of scientific inquiry abilities. *Journal of Research in Science Teaching, 48*(1), 98–116.

ED491D. (n.d.). *Shooting for success! Madelyn Hunter lesson cycle.* Accessed at http://ed491.weebly.com/uploads/8/4/6/1/8461140/anticipatorysets.pdf on April 30, 2015.

Emmer, E. T., Evertson, C. M., & Worsham, M. E. (2003). *Classroom management for secondary teachers* (6th ed.). Boston: Allyn & Bacon.

Endacott, J. L. (2011). Power and liberty: A long-term course planning strategy to encourage the contextualization of events in American history. *Social Studies, 102*(2), 73–79.

English, F. W. (1980). Curriculum mapping. *Educational Leadership, 37*(7), 558–559.

Estes, T. H., Mintz, S. L., & Gunter, M. A. (2010). *Instruction: A models approach* (6th ed.). Boston: Pearson.

Fairris, J. J., Jr. (2008). *The effect degree of curriculum mapping implementation has on student performance levels on sixth and eighth grade benchmark examination.* Unpublished doctoral dissertation, University of Louisiana, Monroe.

Fernandez, C. (2002). Learning from Japanese approaches to professional development: The case of lesson study. *Journal of Teacher Education, 53*(5), 393–405.

Fernandez, C. (2005). Lesson study: A means for elementary teachers to develop the knowledge of mathematics needed for reform-minded teaching. *Mathematical Thinking and Learning, 7*(4), 265–289.

French, L. R., Walker, C. L., & Shore, B. M. (2011). Do gifted students really prefer to work alone? *Roeper Review, 33*(3), 145–159.

Friedman, A. M., & Heafner, T. L. (2008). Finding and contextualizing resources: A digital literacy tool's impact in ninth-grade world history. *Clearing House: A Journal of Educational Strategies, Issues, and Ideas, 82*(2), 82–86.

Fuchs, L. S., Deno, S. L., & Mirkin, P. K. (1984). The effects of frequent curriculum-based measurement and evaluation on pedagogy, student achievement, and student awareness of learning. *American Educational Research Journal, 21*(2), 449–460.

Fuchs, L. S., & Fuchs, D. (2003). *What is scientifically-based research on progress monitoring?* Washington, DC: National Center on Student Progress Monitoring.

Gabric, K. M., Hovance, C. Z., Comstock, S. L., & Harnisch, D. L. (2006). Scientists in their own classroom: The use of Type II technology in the science classroom. *Computers in the Schools, 22*(3–4), 77–91.

Gallagher, S. A., Stepien, W. J., & Rosenthal, H. (1992). The effects of problem-based learning on problem solving. *Gifted Child Quarterly, 36*(4), 195–200.

Gee, J. P. (2003). Opportunity to learn: A language-based perspective on assessment. *Assessment in Education: Principal, Policy, and Practice, 10*(1), 27–46.

Glossary of Education Reform. (2013a, September 16). *Authentic learning.* Accessed at http://edglossary.org /authentic-learning on April 30, 2015.

Glossary of Education Reform. (2013b, August 29). *Relevance.* Accessed at http://edglossary.org/relevance on April 30, 2015.

Goddard, Y. L., Goddard, R. D., & Tschannen-Moran, M. (2007). A theoretical and empirical investigation of teacher collaboration for school improvement and student achievement in public elementary schools. *Teachers College Record, 109*, 877–896.

Goldberg, A., Russell, M., & Cook, A. (2003). The effect of computers on student writing: A meta-analysis of studies from 1992 to 2002. *Journal of Technology, Learning, and Assessment, 2*(1), 1–51. Accessed at https:// ejournals.bc.edu/ojs/index.php/jtla/article/viewFile/1661/1503 on April 30, 2015.

Golden, N., Gersten, R., & Woodward, J. (1990). Effectiveness of guided practice during remedial reading instruction: An application of computer-managed instruction. *Elementary School Journal, 90*(3), 291–304.

Good, T. L., & Brophy, J. E. (2007). *Looking in classrooms* (10th ed.). Boston: Pearson.

Graeff, T. R. (2010). Strategic teaching for active learning. *Marketing Education Review, 20*(3), 265–278.

Graffam, B. (2006). A case study of teachers of gifted learners: Moving from prescribed practices to described practitioners. *Gifted Child Quarterly, 50*(2), 119–131.

Grant, L., Stronge, J., Xu, X., Popp, P., Sun, Y., & Little, C. (2014). *West meets east: Best practices from expert teachers in the U.S. and China.* Alexandria, VA: Association for Supervision and Curriculum Development.

Gronlund, N. E. (2006). *Assessment of student achievement* (8th ed.). Boston: Pearson.

Gulek, J. C., & Demirtas, H. (2005). Learning with technology: The impact of laptop use on student achievement. *Journal of Technology, Learning, and Assessment, 3*(2), 1–38. Accessed at https://ejournals.bc.edu/ojs/index.php/jtla/article/view/1655/1501 on April 30, 2015.

Gupta, A., & Fisher, D. (2012). Technology-supported learning environments in science classrooms in India. *Learning Environments Research, 15*(2), 195–216.

Guzey, S., & Roehrig, G. (2012). Educational technology in a novice science teachers' classroom. In I. L. Chen & D. McPheeters (Eds.), *Cases on educational technology integration in urban schools* (pp. 145–153). Hershey, PA: IGI Global.

Hale, M. S., & City, E. A. (2006). *The teacher's guide to leading student-centered discussions: Talking about texts in the classroom.* Thousand Oaks, CA: Corwin Press.

Hamilton, B. (2007). *It's elementary! Integrating technology in the primary grades.* Eugene, OR: International Society for Technology in Education.

Hammerness, K., Darling-Hammond, L., & Bransford, J. (2005). How teachers learn and develop. In L. Darling-Hammond & J. Bransford (Eds.), *Preparing teachers for a changing world: What teachers should learn and be able to do* (pp. 358–389). San Francisco: Jossey-Bass.

Hansen, J. B., & Feldhusen, J. F. (1994). Comparison of trained and untrained teachers of gifted students. *Gifted Child Quarterly, 38*(3), 115–121.

Harrison, C., Comber, C., Fisher, T., Haw, K., Lewin, C., Lunzer, E., et al. (2002). *ImpaCT2: The impact of information and communication technologies on pupil learning and attainment.* Coventry, England: British Educational Communications and Technology Agency.

Hartley, J., & Davies, I. K. (1976). Preinstructional strategies: The role of pretests, behavioral objectives, overviews, and advance organizers. *Review of Educational Research, 46*(2), 239–265.

Hattie, J. (2009). *Visible learning: A synthesis of over 800 meta-analyses relating to achievement.* New York: Routledge.

Hawkins, V. J. (2009). Barriers to implementing differentiation: Lack of confidence, efficacy, and perseverance. *New England Reading Association Journal, 44*(2), 11–19.

Haynie, G. (2006, April). *Effective biology teaching: A value-added instructional improvement analysis model* (E&R Report No. 05.28). Accessed at http://webarchive.wcpss.net/results/reports/2006/0528biology.pdf on April 30, 2015.

Heacox, D. (2012). *Differentiating instruction in the regular classroom: How to reach and teach all learners* (Updated anniversary ed.). Minneapolis, MN: Free Spirit.

Helterbran, V. (2008). Planning for instruction: Benefits and obstacles of collaboration. *International Journal of Learning, 15*(1), 89–94.

Herrington, J., Reeves, T. C., & Oliver, R. (2010). *A guide to authentic e-learning.* New York: Routledge.

Hockett, J. A. (2009). Curriculum for highly able learners that conforms to general education and gifted education quality indicators. *Journal for the Education of the Gifted, 32*(3), 394–440.

Hockett, J. A., & Doubet, K. J. (2014). Turning on the lights: What pre-assessments can do. *Educational Leadership, 71*(4), 50–54.

Hokanson, B., & Hooper, S. (2011). Integrating technology in classrooms: We have met the enemy, and he is us. In G. J. Anglin (Ed.), *Instructional technology: Past, present, and future* (3rd ed., pp. 137–144). Santa Barbara, CA: Libraries Unlimited.

Huberman, M., Bitter, C., Anthony, J., & O'Day, J. (2014, September). *The shape of deeper learning: Strategies, structures, and cultures in deeper learning network high schools.* Washington, DC: American Institutes for Research.

Hudson, S., Kadan, S., Lavin, K., & Vasquez, T. (2010). *Improving basic math skills using technology*. Action research project, Saint Xavier University, Chicago.

Hug, B., Krajcik, J. S., & Marx, R. W. (2005). Using innovative learning technologies to promote learning and engagement in an urban science classroom. *Urban Education, 40*(4), 446–472.

Hunter, M. (1994). *Enhancing teaching*. New York: Macmillan College.

Hunter, R. (2004). *Mastery teaching*. Thousand Oaks, CA: Corwin Press.

Ibata-Arens, K. C. (2012). Race to the future: Innovations in gifted and enrichment education in Asia, and implications for the United States. *Administrative Sciences, 2*(1), 1–25.

Instructional Assessment Resources. (2011, September 21). *Writing learning objectives*. Accessed at www.utexas.edu /academic/ctl/assessment/iar/students/plan/objectives on April 30, 2015.

Jackson, A. W., & Davis, G. A. (2000). *Turning points 2000: Educating adolescents in the 21st century*. New York: Teachers College Press.

Jacobs, H. H. (Ed.). (1989). *Interdisciplinary curriculum: Design and implementation*. Alexandria, VA: Association for Supervision and Curriculum Development.

Jacobs, H. H. (1997). *Mapping the big picture: Integrating curriculum and assessment K–12*. Alexandria, VA: Association for Supervision and Curriculum Development.

Jacobs, H. H., & Borland, J. H. (1986). The interdisciplinary concept model: Theory and practice. *Gifted Child Quarterly, 30*(4), 159–163.

Jacobson, S. (2011). Leadership effects on student achievement and sustained school success. *International Journal of Educational Management, 25*(1), 33–44.

Jay, J. K. (2002). Points on a continuum: An expert/novice study of pedagogical reasoning. *Professional Educator, 24*(2), 63–74.

Jitendra, A. K., Edwards, L. L., Choutka, C. M., & Treadway, P. S. (2002). A collaborative approach to planning in the content areas for students with learning disabilities: Accessing the general curriculum. *Learning Disabilities Research and Practice, 17*(4), 252–267.

John, P. D. (2006). Lesson planning and the student teacher: Re-thinking the dominant model. *Journal of Curriculum Studies, 38*(4), 483–498.

Johnsen, S. K., & Ryser, G. R. (1996). An overview of effective practices with gifted students in general-education settings. *Journal for the Education of the Gifted, 19*(4), 379–404.

Jones, K. A., Jones, J., & Vermette, P. J. (2011). Six common lesson planning pitfalls: Recommendations for novice educators. *Education, 131*(4), 845–864.

Jong, B., Lin, T., Wu, Y., & Chan, T. (2004). Diagnostic and remedial learning strategy based on conceptual graphs. *Journal of Computer Assisted Learning, 20*(5), 377–386.

Journell, W. (2009). Maximizing the potential of computer-based technology in secondary social studies education. *Social Studies Research and Practice, 4*(1), 56–70.

Kapitzke, C. (2006). Foreword: Rethinking educational technologies as architecture and aesthetics. In S. Y. Tettegah & R. C. Hunter (Eds.), *Technology and education: Issues in administration, policy, and applications in K12 schools* (pp. ix–xii). Bingley, England: Emerald.

Kaplan, R., & Simmons, F. G. (1974). Effects of instructional objectives used as orienting stimuli or as summary/ review upon prose learning. *Journal of Educational Psychology, 66*(4), 614–622.

Kennedy, M. M. (2010). Attribution error and the quest for teacher quality. *Educational Researcher, 39*(8), 591–598.

Kent School District. (n.d.). *K–6 integrated technology units*. Accessed at www1.kent.k12.wa.us/ksd/it/inst_tech /TechClassroom/k6_int_tech.html on April 30, 2015.

Kerr, K. A., Marsh, J. A., Ikemoto, G. S., Darilek, H., & Barney, H. (2006). Strategies to promote data use for instructional improvement: Actions, outcomes, and lessons from three urban districts. *American Journal of Education, 112*(4), 496–520.

Klauer, K. J. (1984). Intentional and incidental learning with instructional texts: A meta-analysis for 1970–1980. *American Educational Research Journal, 21*(2), 323–339.

Ko, E. K. (2012). What is your objective? Preservice teachers' views and practice of instructional planning. *International Journal of Learning, 18*(7), 89–100.

Kounin, J. S. (1977). *Discipline and group management in classrooms.* New York: Holt, Rinehart & Winston.

Lambert, G. E. (1988). Lesson planning and the experienced teacher. *OCSS Review, 24*(1), 52–58.

Lee, S.-Y., Olszewski-Kubilius, P., & Peternel, G. (2010). The efficacy of academic acceleration for gifted minority students. *Gifted Child Quarterly, 54*(3), 189–208.

Lei, J., & Zhao, Y. (2007). Technology uses and student achievement: A longitudinal study. *Computers and Education, 49*(2), 284–296.

Leinhardt, G. (1993). On teaching. In R. Glaser (Ed.), *Advances in instructional psychology* (Vol. 4, pp. 1–54). Hillsdale, NJ: Erlbaum.

LePage, P., Darling-Hammond, L., & Akar, H. (2005). Classroom management. In L. Darling-Hammond & J. Bransford (Eds.), *Preparing teachers for a changing world: What teachers should learn and be able to do* (pp. 327–357). San Francisco: Jossey-Bass.

Levin, T., & Wadmany, R. (2008). Teachers' views on factors affecting effective integration of information technology in the classroom: Developmental scenery. *Journal of Technology and Teacher Education, 16*(2), 233–263.

Levine, T. H., & Marcus, A. S. (2010). How the structure and focus of teachers' collaborative activities facilitate and constrain teacher learning. *Teaching and Teacher Education, 26,* 389–398.

Levstik, L. S., & Barton, K. C. (2005). *Doing history: Investigating with children in elementary and middle schools* (3rd ed.). Mahwah, NJ: Erlbaum.

Lewis, C., Perry, R., & Hurd, J. (2004). A deeper look at lesson study. *Educational Leadership, 61*(5), 18–22.

Lewis, C., Perry, R., & Murata, A. (2006). How should research contribute to instructional improvement? The case of lesson study. *Educational Researcher, 35*(3), 3–14.

Lewis, C., & Tsuchida, I. (1998). A lesson is like a swiftly flowing river: How research lessons improve Japanese education. *American Educator, 22*(4), 12–17, 50–52.

Li, Q., & Ma, X. (2010). A meta-analysis of the effects of computer technology on school students' mathematics learning. *Educational Psychology Review, 22*(3), 215–243.

Liao, Y.-K. C., & Hao, Y. (2008). Large-scale studies and quantitative methods. In J. Voogt & G. Knezek (Eds.), *International handbook of information technology in primary and secondary education* (pp. 1019–1035). New York: Springer.

Lin, C. H., Liu, E. Z. F., Chen, Y. L., Liou, P.-Y., Chang, M., Wu, C. H., et al. (2013). Game-based remedial instruction in mastery learning for upper-primary school students. *Educational Technology and Society, 16*(2), 271–281.

Little, C. A. (2012). Curriculum as motivation for gifted students. *Psychology in the Schools, 49*(7), 695–705.

Liu, M. (2005). The effect of a hypermedia learning environment on middle school students' motivation, attitude, and science knowledge. *Computers in the Schools, 22*(3–4), 159–171.

Livingston, C., & Borko, H. (1989). Expert-novice differences in teaching: A cognitive analysis and implications for teacher education. *Journal of Teacher Education, 40*(4), 36–42.

Lookabill, K. C. (2008). *A descriptive study of the impact of the planning time on the utilization of the National Council of Teachers of Mathematics process standards within the algebra 1 and applied mathematics subject fields.* Unpublished doctoral dissertation, Marshall University, Huntington, West Virginia.

Lopez, R., & MacKenzie, J. (1993). A learning center approach to individualized instruction for gifted students. In C. J. Maker (Ed.), *Critical issues in gifted education: Programs for the gifted in regular classrooms* (pp. 282–295). Austin, TX: PRO-ED.

Lucas, R. M. (2005). *Teachers' perceptions on the efficacy of curriculum mapping as a tool for planning and curriculum alignment.* Unpublished doctoral dissertation, Seton Hall University, South Orange, New Jersey.

Lucero, R. (n.d.). *Closure activities: Making that last impression.* Accessed at http://teaching.colostate.edu/tips/tip .cfm?tipid=148 on April 30, 2015.

Maddux, C. D., & Johnson, D. L. (2006). Information technology, Type II classroom integration, and the limited infrastructure in schools. In C. D. Maddux & D. L. Johnson (Eds.), *Classroom integration of Type II uses of technology in education* (pp. 1–6). New York: Routledge.

Mager, R. F. (1997). *Preparing instructional objectives: A critical tool in the development of effective instruction* (3rd ed.). Atlanta, GA: Center for Effective Performance.

Margolis, H., & McCabe, P. P. (2004). Self-efficacy: A key to improving the motivation of struggling learners. *Clearing House: A Journal of Educational Strategies, Issues, and Ideas, 77*(6), 241–249.

Marzano, R. J., Pickering, D. J., & McTighe, J. (1993). *Assessing student outcomes: Performance assessment using the dimensions of learning model.* Alexandria, VA: Association for Supervision and Curriculum Development.

McCutcheon, G. (1980). How do elementary school teachers plan? The nature of planning and influences on it. *Elementary School Journal, 81*(1), 4–23.

McEwan, E. K. (2002). *Ten traits of highly effective teachers: How to hire, coach, and mentor successful teachers.* Thousand Oaks, CA: Corwin Press.

McLean, A. (2003). *The motivated school.* Thousand Oaks, CA: SAGE.

McMillan, J. H. (2011). *Classroom assessment: Principles and practice for effective standards-based instruction* (5th ed.). Boston: Pearson.

Meirink, J. A., Imants, J., Meijer, P. C., & Verloop, N. (2010). Teacher learning and collaboration in innovative teams. *Cambridge Journal of Education, 40*(2), 161–181.

Melton, R. F. (1978). Resolution of conflicting claims concerning the effect of behavioral objectives on student learning. *Review of Educational Research, 48*(2), 291–302.

Mertens, S. B., Flowers, N., Anfara, V. A., Jr., & Caskey, M. M. (2010). Common planning time. *Middle School Journal, 41*(5), 50–57.

Michaels, C. A., Wilson, G. L., & Margolis, H. (2005). Promoting self-efficacy and academic competency: Instructional implications for struggling secondary learners. In G. D. Sideridis & T. A. Citro (Eds.), *Research to practice: Effective interventions in learning disabilities* (pp. 90–122). Weston, MA: Learning Disabilities Worldwide.

Michelsen, C., & Sriraman, B. (2009). Does interdisciplinary instruction raise students' interest in mathematics and the subjects of the natural sciences? *ZDM: The International Journal on Mathematics Education, 41*(1–2), 231–244.

Miller, S. D. (2003). How high- and low-challenge tasks affect motivation and learning: Implications for struggling learners. *Reading and Writing Quarterly: Overcoming Learning Difficulties, 19*(1), 39–57.

Mishra, P., & Koehler, M. J. (2006). Technological pedagogical content knowledge: A framework for teacher knowledge. *Teachers College Record, 108*(6), 1017–1054.

Misulis, K. (1997). Content analysis: A useful tool for instructional planning. *Contemporary Education, 69*(1), 45–47.

Moolenaar, N. M., Sleegers, P. J. C, & Daly, A. J. (2012). Teaming up: Linking collaboration networks, collective efficacy, and student achievement. *Teaching and Teacher Education, 28*, 251–262.

Moon, S. M., Feldhusen, J. F., & Dillon, D. R. (1994). Long-term effects of an enrichment program based on the Purdue three-stage model. *Gifted Child Quarterly, 38*(1), 38–48.

Moore, K. D. (2005). *Effective instructional strategies: From theory to practice.* Thousand Oaks, CA: SAGE.

Murphy, C. U., & Lick, D. W. (2005). *Whole-faculty study groups: Creating professional learning communities that target student learning* (3rd ed.). Thousand Oaks, CA: Corwin Press.

Natriello, G. (1987). The impact of evaluation processes on students. *Educational Psychologist, 22*(2), 155–175.

Nelson, K. C., & Prindle, N. (1992). Gifted teacher competencies: Ratings by rural principals and teachers compared. *Journal for the Education of the Gifted, 15*(4), 357–369.

Ohio University Heritage College of Osteopathic Medicine. (n.d.). *Writing learning objectives: Beginning with the end in mind.* Accessed at www.oucom.ohiou.edu/fd/writingobjectives.pdf on April 30, 2015.

Olenchak, F. R. (1995). Effects of enrichment on gifted/learning-disabled students. *Journal for the Education of the Gifted, 18*(4), 385–398.

Orlich, D. C., Harder, R. J., Callahan, R. C., Trevisan, M. S., & Brown, A. H. (2009). *Teaching strategies: A guide to effective instruction* (9th ed.). Boston: Cengage Learning.

Ornstein, A. C., & Lasley, T. J., II. (2004). *Strategies for effective teaching* (3rd ed.). Boston: McGraw-Hill.

O'Sullivan, C. Y., Lauko, M. A., Grigg, W. S., Qian, J., & Zhang, J. (2003, January). *The nation's report card: Science 2000* (NCES 2003-453). Washington, DC: U.S. Department of Education, Institute of Education Science, National Center for Education Statistics.

Pahomov, L. (2014). *Authentic learning in the digital age: Engaging students through inquiry.* Alexandria, VA: Association for Supervision and Curriculum Development.

Panasuk, R. M., Stone, W. E., & Todd, J. W. (2002). Lesson planning strategy for effective mathematics teaching. *Education, 122*(4), 808–826.

Panasuk, R. M., & Todd, J. W. (2005). Effectiveness of lesson planning: Factor analysis. *Journal of Instructional Psychology, 32*(3), 215–232.

Park, H., Khan, S., & Petrina, S. (2009). ICT in science education: A quasi-experimental study of achievement, attitudes toward science, and career aspirations of Korean middle school students. *International Journal of Science Education, 31*(8), 993–1012.

Parker, D. (1994). *Every student succeeds: A conceptual framework for students at risk of school failure.* Sacramento, CA: California Department of Education.

Partnership for 21st Century Skills. (2009). *P21 framework definitions.* Accessed at www.p21.org/storage/documents /P21_Framework_Definitions.pdf on April 30, 2015.

Pearson, P. D., Ferdig, R. E., Blomeyer, R. L., Jr., & Moran, J. (2005, November). *The effects of technology on reading performance in the middle-school grades: A meta-analysis with recommendations for policy.* Naperville, IL: Learning Point Associates.

Pennisi, A. C. (2012). A partnership across boundaries: Arts integration in high schools. *Teaching Artist Journal, 10*(2), 102–109.

Piaget, J. (1997). *The origin of intelligence in the child.* London: Routledge.

Pierce, R. L., Cassady, J. C., Adams, C. M., Neumeister, K. L. S., Dixon, F. A., & Cross, T. L. (2011). The effects of clustering and curriculum on the development of gifted learners' math achievement. *Journal for the Education of the Gifted, 34*(4), 569–594.

Pitler, H., Hubbell, E. R., Kuhn, M., & Malenoski, K. (2007). *Using technology with classroom instruction that works.* Alexandria, VA: Association for Supervision and Curriculum Development.

Plewis, I. (1998). Curriculum coverage and classroom grouping as explanations of between teacher differences in pupils' mathematics progress. *Educational Research and Evaluation, 4*(2), 97–107.

Pollock, J. E. (2007). *Improving student learning: One teacher at a time.* Alexandria, VA: Association for Supervision and Curriculum Development.

Preus, B. (2007). Educational trends in China and the United States: Proverbial pendulum or potential for balance? *Phi Delta Kappan, 89*(2), 115–118.

Puckett, K. (2006). An assistive technology toolkit: Type II applications for students with mild disabilities. *Computers in the Schools, 22*(3–4), 107–117.

Reed, D. K. (2012). Clearly communicating the learning objective matters! *Middle School Journal, 43*(5), 16–24.

Reese, T. (2014). Lesson closure: Stick the landing. *Education Update, 56*(6), 5.

Reeves, A. R. (2011). *Where great teaching begins: Planning for student thinking and learning.* Alexandria, VA: Association of Supervision and Curriculum Development.

Reis, S. M., McCoach, D. B., Little, C. A., Muller, L. M., & Kaniskan, R. B. (2011). The effects of differentiated instruction and enrichment pedagogy on reading achievement in five elementary schools. *American Educational Research Journal, 48*(2), 462–501.

Reis, S. M., Westberg, K. L., Kulikowich, J. M., & Purcell, J. H. (1998). Curriculum compacting and achievement test scores: What does the research say? *Gifted Child Quarterly, 42*(2), 123–129.

Riedling, A. M. (2007). *An educator's guide to information literacy: What every high school senior needs to know.* Westport, CT: Libraries Unlimited.

Rimm, S. B., & Lovance, K. J. (1992). The use of subject and grade skipping for the prevention and reversal of underachievement. *Gifted Child Quarterly, 36*(2), 100–105.

Rimpola, R. C. (2014). Collaborative planning and teacher efficacy of high school mathematics co-teachers. *Educational Planning, 21*(3), 41–53.

Robelen, E. W. (2012, November 13). Literacy instruction expected to cross disciplines. *Education Week.* Accessed at www.edweek.org/ew/articles/2012/11/14/12cc-crosscurriculum.h32.html on April 30, 2015.

Roberts, G., Vaughn, S., Fletcher, J., Stuebing, K., & Barth, A. (2013). Effects of a response-based, tiered framework for intervening with struggling readers in middle school. *Reading Research Quarterly, 48*(3), 237–254.

Robinson, A., Shore, B. M., & Enersen, D. L. (2007). *Best practices in gifted education: An evidence-based guide.* Waco, TX: Prufrock Press.

Rosen, Y., & Beck-Hill, D. (2012). Intertwining digital content and a one-to-one laptop environment in teaching and learning: Lessons from the time to know program. *Journal of Research on Technology in Education, 44*(3), 225–241.

Rosenshine, B. V. (1986). Synthesis of research on explicit teaching. *Educational Leadership, 43*(7), 60–69.

Ross, S. M., Morrison, G. R., & Lowther, D. L. (2010). Educational technology research past and present: Balancing rigor and relevance to impact school learning. *Contemporary Educational Technology, 1*(1), 17–35. Accessed at www.cedtech.net/articles/112.pdf on April 30, 2015.

Sabers, D. S., Cushing, K. S., & Berliner, D. C. (1991). Differences among teachers in a task characterized by simultaneity, multidimensionality, and immediacy. *American Educational Research Journal, 28*(1), 63–88.

Safer, N., & Fleischman, S. (2005). How student progress monitoring improves instruction. *Educational Leadership*, *62*(5), 81–83.

Sawyer, R. K. (2011). What makes good teachers great? The artful balance of structure and improvisation. In R. K. Sawyer (Ed.), *Structure and improvisation in creative teaching* (pp. 1–24). New York: Cambridge University Press.

Schmidt, W. H., Cogan, L. S., Houang, R. T., & McKnight, C. C. (2011). Content coverage differences across districts/states: A persisting challenge for U.S. education policy. *American Journal of Education, 117*(3), 399–427.

Schmidt, W. H., Cogan, L. S., & McKnight, C. C. (2010–2011). Equality of educational opportunity: Myth or reality in U.S. schooling? *American Educator, 34*(4), 12–19.

Schmoker, M. (2004). Tipping point: From feckless reform to substantive instructional improvement. *Phi Delta Kappan, 85*(6), 424–432.

Schroeder, C. M., Scott, T. P., Tolson, H., Huang, T.-Y., & Lee, Y.-H. (2007). A meta-analysis of national research: Effects of teaching strategies on student achievement in science in the United States. *Journal of Research in Science Teaching, 44*(10), 1436–1460.

Schumm, J. S., Vaughn, S., Haager, D., McDowell, J., Rothlein, L., & Saumell, L. (1995). General education teacher planning: What can students with learning disabilities expect? *Exceptional Children, 61*(4), 335–352.

Schunk, D. H. (1985). Self-efficacy and classroom learning. *Psychology in the Schools, 22*(2), 208–223.

Shanks, D. J. (2002). *A comparative study on academic gains between students in second grade through sixth grade before and after curriculum mapping.* Unpublished doctoral dissertation, Tennessee State University, Nashville.

Sharma, M. B., & Elbow, G. S. (2000). *Using Internet primary sources to teach critical thinking skills in geography.* Westport, CT: Greenwood Press.

Shield, M., & Dole, S. (2013). Assessing the potential of mathematics textbooks to promote deep learning. *Educational Studies in Mathematics, 82*(2), 183–199.

Shilling, T. (2013). Opportunities and challenges of curriculum mapping implementation in one school setting: Considerations for school leaders. *Journal of Curriculum and Instruction, 7*(2), 20–37.

Shimizu, Y. (2008). Exploring Japanese teachers' conception of mathematics lesson structure: Similarities and differences between pre-service and in-service teachers' lesson plans. *ZDM: The International Journal on Mathematics Education, 40*(6), 941–950.

Shore, B. M., & Delcourt, M. A. B. (1996). Effective curricular and program practices in gifted education and the interface with general education. *Journal for the Education of the Gifted, 20*(2), 138–154.

Shulman, L. S. (1986). Those who understand: Knowledge growth in teaching. *Educational Researcher, 15*(2), 4–14.

Sivin-Kachala, J., Bialo, E., & Rosso, J. L. (2000). *Online and electronic research by middle school students.* Santa Monica, CA: Milken Family Foundation.

Snyder, S. (2001). Connection, correlation, and integration. *Music Educators Journal, 87*(5), 32–40.

Sousa, D. A. (2011). *How the brain learns* (4th ed.). Thousand Oaks, CA: Corwin Press.

Sousa, D. A., & Tomlinson, C. A. (2011). *Differentiation and the brain: How neuroscience supports the learner-friendly classroom.* Bloomington, IN: Solution Tree Press.

Steenbergen-Hu, S., & Moon, S. M. (2011). The effects of acceleration on high-ability learners: A meta-analysis. *Gifted Child Quarterly, 55*(1), 39–53.

Stewart, R. A., & Brendefur, J. L. (2005). Fusing lesson study and authentic achievement: A model for teacher collaboration. *Phi Delta Kappan, 86*(9), 681–687.

Stiggins, R., & DuFour, R. (2009). Maximizing the power of formative assessments. *Phi Delta Kappan, 90*(9), 640–644.

Stigler, J. W., & Hiebert, J. (1999). *The teaching gap: Best ideas from the world's teachers for improving education in the classroom.* New York: Free Press.

Stols, G. (2013). An investigation into the opportunity to learn that is available to grade 12 mathematics learners. *South African Journal of Education, 33*(1), 1–18.

Stripling, B. K. (Ed.). (1999). *Learning and libraries in an information age: Principles and practice.* Englewood, CO: Libraries Unlimited.

Stronge, J. H. (2007). *Qualities of effective teachers* (2nd ed.). Alexandria, VA: Association for Supervision and Curriculum Development.

Stronge, J. H., & Grant, L. W. (2013). *Student achievement goal setting: Using data to improve teacher and learning.* New York: Routledge.

Stronge, J. H., Little, C. A., & Grant, L. W. (2009). Qualities of talented teachers: Reflections and new directions. In B. MacFarlane & T. Stambaugh (Eds.), *Leading change in gifted education: The festschrift of Dr. Joyce Van Tassel-Baska* (pp. 389–401). Waco, TX: Prufrock Press.

Swan, K., Cook, D., Kratcoski, A., Lin, Y. M., Schenker, J., & van't Hooft, M. (2006). Ubiquitous computing: Rethinking teaching, learning, and technology integration. In S. Y. Tettegah & R. C. Hunter (Eds.), *Technology and education: Issues in administration, policy, and applications in K12 schools* (pp. 231–252). Bingley, England: Emerald.

Tally, B., & Goldenberg, L. B. (2005). Fostering historical thinking with digitized primary sources. *Journal of Research on Technology in Education, 38*(1), 1–21.

Tamim, R. M., Bernard, R. M., Borokhovski, E., Abrami, P. C., & Schmid, R. F. (2011). What forty years of research says about the impact of technology on learning: A second-order meta-analysis and validation study. *Review of Educational Research, 81*(1), 4–28.

Teacher Tap. (n.d.). *Evaluating Internet resources.* Accessed at http://eduscapes.com/tap/topic32.htm on April 30, 2015.

Thapa, A., Cohen, J., Guffey, S., & Higgins-D'Alessandro, A. (2013). A review of school climate research. *Review of Educational Research, 83*(3), 357–385.

Thompson, D. R., Kaur, B., Koyama, M., & Bleiler, S. K. (2013). A longitudinal view of mathematics achievement of primary students: Case studies from Japan, Singapore, and the United States. *ZDM: The International Journal on Mathematics Education, 45*(1), 73–89.

Tomlinson, C. A. (1999). *The differentiated classroom: Responding to the needs of all learners.* Alexandria, VA: Association for Supervision and Curriculum Development.

Tomlinson, C. A. (2014). *The differentiated classroom: Responding to the needs of all learners* (2nd ed.). Alexandria, VA: Association for Supervision and Curriculum Development.

Tomlinson, C. A., & Imbeau, M. B. (2010). *Leading and managing: A differentiated classroom.* Alexandria, VA: Association for Supervision and Curriculum Development.

Torgerson, C. J., & Elbourne, D. (2002). A systematic review and meta-analysis of the effectiveness of information and communication technology (ICT) on the teaching of spelling. *Journal of Research in Reading, 25*(2), 129–143.

Torrez, C. A. (2010). "Because I was curious": Oral histories and Web 2.0 in elementary social studies methods. *International Journal of Technology in Teaching and Learning, 6*(2), 146–156.

Torrez, C. F., & Waring, S. M. (2009). Elementary school students, artifacts and primary sources: Learning to engage in historical inquiry. *Social Studies Research and Practice, 4*(2), 79–86.

Tsui, A. B. M., & Wong, J. L. N. (2009). In search of a third space: Teacher development in mainland China. In C. K. K. Chan & N. Rao (Eds.), *Revisiting the Chinese learner: Changing contexts, changing education* (pp. 281–311). Hong Kong, China: Comparative Education Research Centre.

Tucker, P. D., & Stronge, J. H. (2005). *Linking teacher evaluation and student learning.* Alexandria, VA: Association for Supervision and Curriculum Development.

Tuttle, H. G. (2008). Technology = math success. *Technology and Learning, 28*(7), 30.

Tyler, R. W. (1969). *Basic principles of curriculum and instruction.* Chicago: University of Chicago Press.

Usher, E. L. (2009). Sources of middle school students' self-efficacy in mathematics: A qualitative investigation. *American Educational Research Journal, 46*(1), 275–314.

Usher, E. L., & Pajares, F. (2009). Sources of self-efficacy in mathematics: A validation study. *Contemporary Educational Psychology, 34*(1), 89–101.

Vahey, P., Rafanan, K., Patton, C., Swan, K., van't Hooft, M., Kratcoski, A., et al. (2012). A cross-disciplinary approach to teaching data literacy and proportionality. *Educational Studies in Mathematics, 81*(2), 179–205.

Vang, C. T. (2006). New pedagogical approaches for teaching elementary science to limited English proficient students. *Multicultural Education, 13*(3), 37–41.

VanTassel-Baska, J. (1994). *Comprehensive curriculum for gifted learners* (2nd ed.). Boston: Allyn & Bacon.

VanTassel-Baska, J. (2002). *Curriculum planning and instructional design for gifted learners.* Denver, CO: Love.

VanTassel-Baska, J., & Brown, E. F. (2007). Toward best practice: An analysis of the efficacy of curriculum models in gifted education. *Gifted Child Quarterly, 51*(4), 342–358.

VanTassel-Baska, J., & Little, C. A. (Eds.). (2003). *Content-based curriculum for high-ability learners.* Waco, TX: Prufrock Press.

Veltri, N. F., Webb, H. W., Harold, W., Matveev, A. G., & Zapatero, E. G. (2011). Curriculum mapping as a tool for continuous improvement of IS curriculum. *Journal of Information Systems Education, 22*(1), 31–42.

Vygotsky, L. S. (1978). *Mind in society: The development of higher psychological processes.* Cambridge, MA: Harvard University Press.

Waddoups, G. L. (2004). *Technology integration, curriculum, and student achievement: A review of scientifically-based research and implications for EasyTech* [Executive summary]. Portland, OR: Learning.com.

Walker, A., & Pilkington, R. M. (2005). Using computers to assist in developing key literacy skills. In M. Monteith (Ed.), *Teaching secondary school literacies* (pp. 71–96). New York: McGraw-Hill.

Walsh, R. L., Kemp, C. R., Hodge, K. A., & Bowes, J. M. (2012). Searching for evidence-based practice: A review of the research on educational interventions for intellectually gifted children in the early childhood years. *Journal for the Education of the Gifted, 35*(2), 103–128.

Warren, L. L., & Payne, B. D. (1997). Impact of middle grades' organization on teacher efficacy and environmental perceptions. *Journal of Educational Research, 90*(5), 301–308.

Webb, M. E. (2005). Affordances of ICT in science learning: Implications for an integrated pedagogy. *International Journal of Science Education, 27*(6), 705–735.

Wenglinsky, H. (2004). Closing the racial achievement gap: The role of reforming instructional practices. *Education Policy Analysis Archives, 12*(64), 1–22. Accessed at http://epaa.asu.edu/ojs/article/view/219/345 on April 30, 2015.

Westberg, K. L., & Archambault, F. X., Jr. (1997). A multi-site case study of successful classroom practices for high ability students. *Gifted Child Quarterly, 41*(1), 42–51.

Wharton-McDonald, R., Pressley, M., & Hampston, J. M. (1998). Literacy instruction in nine first-grade classrooms: Teacher characteristics and student achievement. *Elementary School Journal, 99*(2), 101–128.

Wiggins, G. (2010). What's my job? Defining the role of the classroom teacher. In R. J. Marzano (Ed.), *On excellence in teaching* (pp. 7–30). Bloomington, IN: Solution Tree Press.

Wiggins, G., & McTighe, J. (1998). *Understanding by design.* Alexandria, VA: Association for Supervision and Curriculum Development.

Wiggins, G., & McTighe, J. (2005). *Understanding by design* (Expanded 2nd ed.). Alexandria, VA: Association for Supervision and Curriculum Development.

Williams, D. G., Carr, T. L., & Clifton, N. S. (2006). Technology and urban youth: Emergent issues regarding access. In S. Y. Tettegah & R. C. Hunter (Eds.), *Technology and education: Issues in administration, policy, and applications in K12 schools* (pp. 101–113). Bingley, England: Emerald.

Wingert, J. R., Wasileski, S. A., Peterson, L., Mathews, L. G., Lanou, A. J., & Clarke, D. (2011). Enhancing integrative experiences: Evidence of student perceptions of learning gains from cross-course interactions. *Journal of the Scholarship of Teaching and Learning, 11*(3), 34–57.

WriteSteps. (n.d.). *Closure activities*. Accessed at www.writestepswriting.com/Portals/0/newsletters/pdf/Closure _Activities.pdf on April 30, 2015.

Yinger, R. J. (1980). A study of teacher planning. *Elementary School Journal, 80*(3), 107–127.

Yorks, P. M., & Follo, E. J. (1993). *Engagement rates during thematic and traditional instruction*. Accessed at http:// files.eric.ed.gov/fulltext/ED363412.pdf on April 30, 2015. (ED363412)

Young, V. M., & Kim, D. H. (2010). Using assessments for instructional improvement: A literature review. *Education Policy Analysis Archives, 18*(19), 1–36. Accessed at http://epaa.asu.edu/ojs/article/view/809 on April 30, 2015.

Zahorik, J., Halbach, A., Ehrle, K., & Molnar, A. (2003). Teaching practices for smaller classes. *Educational Leadership, 61*(1), 75–77.

Zheng, B., Warschauer, M., & Farkas, G. (2013). Digital writing and diversity: The effects of school laptop programs on literacy processes and outcomes. *Journal of Educational Computing Research, 48*(3), 267–299.

Index

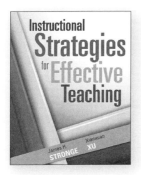

Instructional Strategies for Effective Teaching
James H. Stronge and Xianxuan Xu
Discover research-based instructional strategies teachers, coaches, and administrators can use to enhance their everyday practices. Organized around ten methods of instruction, this user-friendly guide will help you dig deep into classroom discussion, concept mapping, inquiry-based learning, and more.
BKF641

Instructional Methods for Differentiation & Deeper Learning
James H. Stronge and Xianxuan Xu
Discover research-based strategies for differentiated instruction that teachers, coaches, and administrators can use to enhance their everyday practices. Explore ways to implement differentiated learning for students needing personalized remedial instruction and high-ability students, as well as tactics for executing instruction in culturally diverse classrooms.
BKF700

Building a Common Core-Based Curriculum
Susan Udelhofen
Explore various stages of curriculum development, from the preliminary work of building academic support to creating curriculum maps and tracking improvement goals. Learn to effectively share information during the curriculum-building process, and engage in significant, collaborative conversations around the curriculum.
BKF549

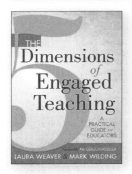

The 5 Dimensions of Engaged Teaching
Laura Weaver and Mark Wilding
Engaged teaching recognizes that educators need to offer more than lesson plans and assessments for students to thrive in the 21st century. Equip your students to be resilient individuals able to communicate effectively and work with diverse people.
BKF601

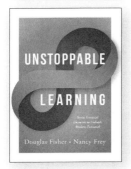

Unstoppable Learning
Douglas Fisher and Nancy Frey
Discover how systems thinking can enhance teaching and learning schoolwide. Examine how to use systems thinking—which involves distinguishing patterns and considering short- and long-term consequences—to better understand the big picture of education and the intricate relationships that impact classrooms. Identify strategies and tools to create clear learning targets, prepare effective lessons, and successfully assess instruction.
BKF662

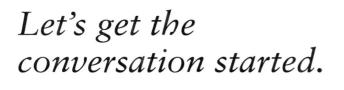